GRANITE GRUMBLINGS

GRANITE GRUMBLINGS

Life in the
"Live Free or Die" State

Observations & Photographs by

Glenn K. Currie

Snap Screen Press
CONCORD, NEW HAMPSHIRE

ISBN 978-0-9779675-3-7
Library of Congress Control Number: 2011903790

Designed and composed in Whitman (11.5/14.5)
with ITC Franklin Gothic display at
Hobblebush Books, Brookline, New Hampshire
www.hobblebush.com

Printed in the United States of America

All photographs in text by Glenn K. Currie
Dustjacket author photo by Susanne G. Currie

Published by:
Snap Screen Press
6 Dwinell Drive
Concord, NH 03301

For more information, visit the website at:
www.snapscreenpress.com
or e-mail: glenn.snapscreen@gmail.com

Contents

Introduction

THE ENCLOSED OBSERVATIONS were written over the last twenty years. Several have never been previously published. Many of the others were first seen in the *Concord Monitor* and the *Sunday Monitor*, where I have been a contributor during those years. A few were first published in *New Hampshire Magazine* and the *New Hampshire Union Leader.*

These pages incorporate a mix of humor and a more introspective look at some of the things that have made New Hampshire and Concord special places to live. Some of these qualities include the independence of our citizens, our ability to laugh at ourselves, and the secure knowledge that New Hampshire has things figured out better than the rest of the country. Many of the subjects are what we sit around and discuss with each other at morning coffee or dinner parties.

Despite the great blessing of living here, my friends tell me that I complain a lot, which is true. But I have found that if I do it with humor, I can usually get away with it. And my complaints are really about trying to make us even better. It is also an effort to help cure newcomers of potentially bad habits, especially if they have just moved up from Massachusetts.

This collection is a reflection of one man's journey through two decades of living in New Hampshire. I hope it provides some smiles, and also some thoughtful moments, about the meaning of living in the "Live Free or Die" state.

Acknowledgments

I would like to thank the *Concord Monitor* and *New Hampshire Magazine* (where several of these segments were first published) for their support and patience with me during our professional associations. It has been a genuine pleasure to work with the personnel at these fine publications.

I would also like to thank my family for the moral support, occasional technical assistance (Lara), and for being agreeable to serve as photographic subject matter for some of these segments (even when they were a little embarrassing).

Many thanks to Sid Hall at Hobblebush Books for book design, typesetting, editing and printing, and also to Town and Country Reprographics (Danyelle) for digital conversion of some of my photos.

Finally, I would like to thank my readers for their sustained interest and encouragement in my efforts. This book would not have happened without them.

—Glenn K. Currie

Phil and Larry's

WHEN PHIL AND LARRY'S store closed, it marked the passing of an institution which had been a landmark for the community. It was a destination for countless high school students who appreciated its convenience to their classrooms, but even more, it was the sustaining energy for a neighborhood.

During the lifetime of this business, the world changed. Small downtowns were assaulted by the encroachment of mammoth malls. Service stations became convenience stores with self-service gas pumps. Five and dime stores gave way to Walmart and Target, and the corner grocer traded his apron for the unreadable name tag of the supermarket.

Somewhere along the way, the sense of ourselves as individuals also started to disappear, burning out in the white-hot intensity of modern life. People rushed, head down, from door to car to door, consumed by the demands of making a living, and content to satisfy their needs for conversation and human contact through the sanitized filter of the TV screen and the internet. Along the way, friends became acquaintances, neighbors were hardly known, and parents and children sometimes became distant relatives.

There were few lifelines to reach for as the waves of change swept us along. The banker who used to work on a handshake, suddenly was replaced by someone reporting to Boston or Ireland, and needed a file to know your name. And the family doctor was often replaced by organizations that ran on acronyms and numbers.

Maybe that's why the passing of Phil Denoncourt's little store had such a profound affect on the community it served. Phil is a personable man who seemed to reflect the best of old New Hampshire. He looked you in the eye, had that dry sense of humor that seems to be nursed to perfection in this state, and he knew everyone's names. He treated his customers with respect and had the time to listen when you wanted to talk. He and his family provided an environment that made people want to linger and chat after they made their purchases.

Often, when times were slow, you would see Phil and customers playing cribbage or checkers or cards. He was always willing to give you an opinion on the movies in his video library, or discuss the virtues of the local sports teams, many of which he saw up close in his capacity as a baseball and softball umpire.

The store itself had a special charm. It was filled with all sorts of novelty candies, sports cards, and inexpensive toys that made it a joy for children of all ages. You could buy night crawlers, hunting and fishing licenses, hardware items, lottery tickets, or get your skates sharpened. We were often amazed at the variety of items in the store, although I must admit that some of them had been there a while. But more than once when we had searched every store in town in vain for a desperately needed item, we would finally find it on a back shelf at Phil's.

When the world finally left the little store behind, it was because people no longer had time for it. Life had moved to the turnpikes and the country roads had become curiosities.

There was a farewell party at the store, and a final auction attended by friends. Typically, Phil felt he had recouped his inventory costs during the "going out of business" sale that preceded it, so he donated the auction proceeds to charity. People came from all over Concord to laugh and cry and pay their respects. And Phil and his mother and the rest of the family that had seen it through two generations, watched it finally end. A place that had once been called the "city hall annex" because so many of the city's leaders congregated there, finally became an empty shell.

I don't worry about Phil. He had a new job within two days of starting his search. And he is the kind of individual who brings to an employer much more in value than a paycheck can ever return.

I do worry about the community, however. I feel sorry for the high school students who will grow up never experiencing the difference between a Phil and Larry's, and a self-service convenience store. And I grieve for the local residents, present and future, who have lost the chance to meet their neighbors there, talk sports and politics, and feel the pulse of a real neighborhood.

For all of us, these kinds of places were an important part of what shaped the character of New Hampshire, and they are now rapidly disappearing from the scene. ◆

Canoe Trip

THE CANOE LAY ON ITS SIDE, leaning against an old maple that had covered the ground around it with the remains of another autumn. It was a tired traveler that had probably found a final resting place.

I see it whenever I look out the back window and across the pond to Mark's house. It is a tangible reminder of the trip we took down the river a few Octobers ago.

Mark is one of those people who adds a certain extra zest to life. He always seems to have some plan or scheme that he is incubating, and he emanates an optimistic life force that is infectious. His energy and enthusiasm have helped build a softball field and replace the weather-vane on the old fire station, and now he is working to help save the city's theater for the performing arts. He also has many plans and projects that should never see the light of day.

One of the reasons that we get along is that we cover the flip sides of ideas and issues pretty well. He will come over with his latest concept and I'll attempt to pragmatically assess the chances of success. I have signed up for several of these projects, but most of the time, we give the idea a decent burial and wind up having a beer and watching a football game.

The canoe trip resulted from one of these visits early on a Saturday morning. It was a beautiful late fall day and there was an overwhelming urge to get outside and enjoy it before we were covered by the long winter.

Mark said he had checked out a pleasant little section of the Merrimack River that would give us a chance to see Concord from a different perspective. He indicated that he knew right where to put in and take out and that we could make the whole trip in three or four hours.

Now it was my turn. We didn't have any adult life preservers, just floater cushions. (Our pond is only three feet deep.)I hadn't been on a canoe trip in thirty years. The canoe was overweight and out of shape (like us) and wallowed like a pig. None of this hit a target. He assured me that it was a very gentle part of the river and that we could stay close to shore. Besides, this was probably the last good day of the year.

My heart really wasn't into fighting it. I wanted to be outdoors and it sounded like fun. This was part of the reason I had moved back to New England.

We drove north about six miles to a gently graded slope that was ideal for putting in the canoe. I knelt down and put my hand in the water. My fingers started turning numb and I quickly removed them. As I flexed to restore circulation, I watched branches and leaves being swept along at a pretty crisp pace. The river lapped the bank right at the grass line, an indication of the heavy rains we had the previous week.

The day was glorious. Fresh blue skies set off the brown and gold of the land in a brilliant contrast. Along the western horizon there were just the faintest touches of feather clouds.

I was seduced by the day. Little alarm bells were going off all around me, but I was sleeping in the sunshine. Mark wobbled up into the bow of the canoe and sat down. I pushed off and we were on our way, moving quickly down river as the embankments rose up around us. The floater cushions and a six-pack of beer accompanied us on the journey. I did note that, fully loaded as we were, we had about three inches of freeboard and the canoe was handling like a scow.

As the current carried us along, it quickly became apparent that Mark had not spent his life on the water. I knew it was a mistake, and also a little late, but I decided to ask him how many times he had been in a canoe. Without looking back, he responded "You mean counting this?" The correct answer turned out to be two, and the other time was on a pond.

Overhead, a V-shaped phalanx of geese noisily crossed the river and headed south, their chatter the universal language of backseat drivers.

It was at about this point that I realized I hadn't fulfilled my part of the job. We should have been sitting home watching football.

Within half a mile, the water began picking up its pace and I could hear a faint roaring in the distance. When I asked Mark if he heard it, he mentioned the part about the dam. He does that sometimes. He neglects to discuss some details of the plan. The detail this morning was Sewalls Falls Dam. This is an old abandoned dam from the textile mill days that had been partially washed away in one of the big floods, leaving a narrow opening for the river to pass through near the northeastern bank.

In physics we used to study how the speed of water molecules increases when water moves from a wider to a narrower opening. This place would make a great field study for that theory.

As we came around the bend and got our first look at the opening, I could see the water splashing 15–20 feet in the air as it crashed over the rocks and raced through the opening. I watched a small log hit one of the rocks and do a vertical 360-degree spin before diving out of sight behind the dam. There were no signs anywhere of other human beings. There was just us and the river.

Mark, as usual, was ready to go for it. We were still several hundred yards from the dam, and I don't think, at that point, he fully appreciated the force that rapids can exert. I replied that they would probably never even find our bodies. As I pointed us toward the shore, I splashed a little of the cold water on him with my paddle.

Neither of us was looking forward to carrying our transportation over what remained of the dam. But by the time we pulled the canoe out of the water and started our portage, we were close enough to the opening to feel the raw power and realize that given our level of canoe incompetence and lack of preparedness, we had made the right decision.

As we wrestled the overweight excuse for a canoe over the trestles, exposed bolts and uncertain footing of the old dam, we stopped a couple of times to lighten our six-pack load. When we finally reached the quiet pool below the dam, I had mellowed out considerably.

As we sat by the canoe building our resolve to continue the voyage, I noticed two crows resting on the branch of a dead tree about twenty yards away. They seemed to stare at us contemptuously for several seconds, before lifting off and lazily heading south. The tree itself, long stripped of bark, suddenly looked naked and forlorn as it hung precariously above the river. It seemed that it would soon be making its own journey.

The rest of the trip down to the arena boat landing was a quiet, easy run. The backyards and floodplains drifted by like a series of Kodachrome posters. The faint hum of traffic on the turnpike provided quiet background music to the river's strange beauty. We saw the remains of old structures that once depended on the river for their life, and newer buildings that turned their backs to the water, exposing only their naked functions. We passed old tires, and clothes and other remnants of people's lives that had been left hanging like cheap necklaces around shrubs and trees neighboring the water. And we paddled through miles of beautiful and untouched land that embraced the river and shared its life.

It was a sobering and enlightening journey that brought us into closer touch with an area that we had never seen. And in the quiet retrospective of the last part of the journey, we could feel the presence of the ghosts that ride the river. Ghosts that beckoned to us, extending the sweet seduction of blue sky and sunlight, while hiding below in the moody blackness. ◆

Author's note: This trip was taken in 1991 before the opening at Sewalls Falls Dam was widened significantly by a subsequent flood.

How Ya Doin' Coach

MANAGING A LITTLE LEAGUE TEAM is a little like getting a wisdom tooth extracted. You're there because you didn't know when to keep your mouth shut. The experience can cause a lot of headaches. And any wisdom acquired in the process will fit neatly in a thimble.

Managing a girl's team is like having the operation without novocaine.

I managed a girl's softball team in the Little League system for five years. I am now in my third year of therapy. I have found that the best treatment is to go to games as a spectator and watch the kids drive someone else nuts.

As part of the recovery program, I thought it might be useful to share the half thimbleful of knowledge that I acquired during those years.

The first rule of coaching is to never expect any gratitude for what you are doing. You will work with some very talented kids. Some may even go on to play on state or regional championship teams. None of these kids will recall any specific softball-related skills that you taught them. The movie screenplays about the star who comes back and thanks the old coach are pretty much fairy tales.

You will be remembered, and you might even be in the movie, but not necessarily the way you would like. The memories of a kid's first coach are more likely to be as the guy with the big butt who wore double knits to practice, or the one who crossed his eyes after getting nailed by the groin-high line drive while pitching batting practice. You may run across some of your players in later years and they will probably come over to say hello, but mostly the discussion will be about how old you look.

So when those fresh-faced little darlings come to their first practice thinking a softball is really soft, don't console yourself with dreams of later glory. You are just somebody who brings the equipment.

The first practice I ever held nearly decimated my team. I pulled out a bucket of balls and asked the kids to split up in pairs and play catch. Within seconds, balls were flying everywhere. Most were not caught and traveled until they hit something. Fortunately, most of them couldn't throw either, so the damage was minimal. I quickly realized that if I had them line up parallel to each other, the misses would be less exciting. I also learned that you never let two close friends line up next to each other. An absolute certainty of girls playing catch is that one will always turn her head to talk to a friend just as the other end of the catching tandem has launched her best throw of the week.

This brings up a key coaching rule. Always have plenty of those chemical ice packs available. No matter what minor trauma happens to a kid, the ice packs seem to work. Bumps, bruises, sprains, strains, even blows to the psyche are all dealt with in a reasonable, efficient manner with these wonderful little bags. I would caution, however, to practice a few times in private before you try to activate the things. I have seen coaches out on the field banging a bag with a baseball bat to activate the chemicals. This does not provide a calming atmosphere for a crying ten-year-old, and doesn't do much for the parents in the stands either.

A corollary to this rule is to keep the girls away from these bags in the hot weather. Otherwise your cold pack budget is going through the roof.

Coaching girl's softball also requires flexibility. You will find that most of the girls are not planning to become Olympic players. They have many other pressing interests such as ballet, band, cheerleading, piano lessons, school plays, gymnastics, walking the dog or the boy friend, and shopping. All of these will be used as excuses for missing practices, particularly on hot days. Don't let this get you too upset. Remember, you are just the guy who brings the equipment.

The key to succeeding as a coach is to learn to think like the kids. This requires careful study of the mind of a ten-year-old. Never anticipate what they will do on the field, especially in a game. It will lead to disappointment and spoil the adventure. Also don't ever use signals with the young kids unless you are trying to confuse the enemy coach. Any signals that they can understand will be so simple that everyone on the field will know what you've called. Everyone except the kid. I have found that whispering the play into the kid's ear can be slightly more effective, although even here you must be careful.

I once pulled a girl aside and told her to take a strike when she got up. I then called time just before she stepped into the batter's box and told her once again to take the first strike. She then proceeded to swing at the first three pitches, all of which were at least a foot over her head. When she strolled dejectedly back to the dugout I asked her in my most restrained and calming voice, why she hadn't taken a strike. She gave me one of those looks like I had just fallen off the turnip truck, and said, "None of them were strikes."

As a manager, I found that I spent most of my time repeating myself. When discussing rules, fielding, hitting or base running, it usually works best to look each kid in the eye and repeat the point at least three times in a loud voice. Always do this at a practice where everybody else is also crowded around listening. Repeat this eyeball to eyeball procedure with everyone in the group, That way, if you have twelve kids at practice, you will have repeated the point thirty-six times. This will assure that maybe one-third of the team will get the message.

Remember, during a game, do not try to teach the kids anything. You will go hoarse, the parents will think you are yelling at the kid, and the girls, occupied by the crowd, and the thrill of the moment, won't be listening anyway.

Pay attention to the helmet rule. Never send a kid out to coach a base without one. And be aware that they will forget their helmet at least fifty percent of the time. This is a rule based on years of experience. A kid as a base coach is out there to smile at the crowd, draw little pictures in the dirt, or sulk because she is not playing. The only advice she will give a runner is whether her pants are dirty. She will not see the wild throw coming to first and without a helmet will be a candidate for an ice pack.

Let the kids have a little freedom to be inventive on the field. I used to tell my base runners to be aggressive. This usually meant for them to run until the umpires made them stop. Not only did this provide lots of exercise for my players, but often resulted in causing the other team to throw the ball all over the field, accounting for most of our runs. On defense, when the other team did this to us, the kids developed a strategy whereby the player with the best arm threw the ball out of bounds. The umpires were then duty bound to stop the races and only allow everyone one or two bases. This was often a moral victory.

As a manager, it is easy to occasionally get frustrated. After all, you are supposed to be in charge of a situation which is often totally out of control. You're dealing with parents who consider you a glorified baby-sitter, kids who think you're a relic from the dark ages, and umpires who are not interested in what you think.

Every once in a while you will see the pressures become too much. I once watched as an opposing manager threw everything in his equipment bag onto the field because he objected to a called third strike. The score was about 42 to 12 and there had been at least thirty-five walks in the game. A called strike was indeed a rarity, but everyone in the park was praying for outs of any kind so that they could get their kids home before midnight. My personal feeling is that the guy was hoping to get thrown out of the game so he wouldn't have to watch it anymore.

At the other end of the spectrum was a manager who didn't last out a year. He was so into the competition that he wanted to play a game when only six of his kids showed up. He tried to talk the opposing manager (me) into letting his team play with three imaginary players. He went so far (I swear this is true) as to put a helmet up at the plate and tell me to have my pitcher pitch to it.

I could go on but I think everyone is getting the picture. The world is a tough place, but the world of managing is even tougher. To be successful, you must keep things in perspective. When you step on that first practice field remember to stock plenty of aspirin (for yourself) and plenty of ice packs. And never forget that you are just the guy who brings the equipment. ◆

Comments from the HHA (Home Health Agency) Frontlines

I SAT IN WHAT I HOPED looked like a state of contemplative evaluation. Actually, however, it was dazed incomprehension.

They were talking about Groupers, HIPPS, No-RAP LUPA's and OASIS.

I hate acronyms. They are never what they seem, and they make my head ache. In fact, lately, the whole health care system is starting to make me crazy.

A few years ago, I agreed to serve on the board of trustees of the Concord Regional Visiting Nurse Association (aka the CRVNA or VNA).

I figured this might be fun. You know, get to meet a lot of nice nurses, eat some cookies at the meetings, maybe learn something about the caregivers who are going to be dealing with me in a few years. (Maybe sooner if there are many more meetings like this one).

The CFO is now discussing HHRG's. "An HHRG of C2FZS1 would have a care mix weight of 1.0758 and a labor quotient of 1.3303, if the patient lives in Barnstable . . . "

The room begins to swim. A bunch of old Navy acronyms suddenly appear on the inside of my eyeballs (MEGO/SOS/ASAP). I have a page and a half of these VNA acronyms and their meanings in front of me, but they aren't helping.

I look up Grouper, which I always thought was a large bottom-feeding fish. But no, according to my sheet, it's "a software module . . . and for HH PPS data from the OASIS assessment tool is grouped to form HHRG's and output HIPPS codes."

It goes downhill from there. Trust me when I tell you that HIPPS and OASIS are not body parts or a green spot in the desert. And the No-RAP LUPAs are not a Latin American singing group.

No wonder Newt wanted to let the Health Care Financing Authority (HCFA), not Medicare, "wither on the vine." This is a bureaucracy that could easily drive me around the bend, and I only have to deal with this stuff twice a month.

The amazing thing to me is that the nurses and administrators actually understand all this stuff. (They don't necessarily like it but they understand it.)

The health care system is getting so complicated now, that only geniuses should apply to become nurses. Which is probably why we have a current shortage of nurses.

Who would have thought twenty years ago that nurses would all be using laptops on their visits, and focusing on POC's, PEP's and PPS to keep HCFA happy.

The good news is that they haven't forgotten about the basic mission of providing quality care to those in need. And despite all the bureaucracy, the level of services that these wonderful people provide is better than ever.

That doesn't, however, prevent me from increasingly feeling like an anachronism in this era of acronyms and anomalies.

I think they just keep me around because I'm so good looking, and I make everyone else feel smart.

(By the way, I am actually writing this in the meeting. Hopefully, all the other trustees and staff think I am paying attention to my DMERC's and SCICs and am just taking copious notes.) ◆

Observations from the Friendly Skies

A GREAT MANY PEOPLE are still afraid to fly after the events of September 11th. Since I have just returned from a trip to Colorado and Texas that involved taking five flights, I thought it might be useful to update everyone on my observations.

First of all, I would like to reassure all of you that there is some good news out there. The airlines have apparently decided to finally take a major step in improving the health and well-being of their passengers. They have stopped serving food on their flights. At least those that I was on.

That's right, you will no longer be assaulted by soggy sandwich rolls that stick to your fingers when you pick them up, and salad dressing packets that spew foul liquids across two rows. And the green eggs that move around, even when there is no turbulence, no longer adorn your food tray early in the morning, when your defenses are at their weakest.

Not only was this considered a major passenger safety move, but it is also apparently saving the airlines money. I know that most of you suspected, as did I, that this food was provided free by the makers of the ever-present airsick bags, but I have been informed by a reliable source that the airlines actually paid for that stuff.

The airsick bag makers should not give up hope, however, because even though the airlines say that they no longer serve food, they do serve little bags of something they call "party mix." A quick check of the list of ingredients indicated that this contains, among other things, disodium phosphate, TBHQ, malic acid, dextrose monohydrate, silica gel anticaking agent, turmeric and, not surprisingly, sodium bicarbonate.

There is more good news. People don't appear to be talking to strangers as much. This should reduce your chances of sitting next to some obnoxious creep who wants to fill you in on the eating habits of his pet anaconda. Instead everyone is keeping at arms length in case they are required to fight their seat mate to the death in mid-flight. A girl came aboard in platform shoes on one flight, and I could see several people mentally calculating how many pounds of plastic explosive she could have been wearing. Any sudden moves and that young lady would have been toast.

My particular airline has also made it more difficult for potential terrorists by instituting a diabolical security plan involving a restructuring of its seating. There was, at most, an inch of free space between my knees and the seat in front of me. If that seat was reclined, I had to move my knees to my chest or risk amputation. I was told that there was an emergency plan that called for the flight attendant to instruct all passengers to recline their seats simultaneously. This would immediately immobilize any terrorists, preventing them from setting off shoe bombs, and rendering them unable to make any other threatening movements.

While I can understand the usefulness of this ploy, I must confess that I was actually driven to thoughts of violence when the passenger in front of me on one flight executed an unexpected emergency seat recline while I was having my coffee and "party mix." He was truly fortunate that I couldn't reach my dental floss, and that the hot liquid leaking toward my crotch quickly reordered my priorities.

I also would like to report that although the security lines can sometimes be quite long, you should approach it as a rare opportunity to interact with your fellow man. It is a little bothersome to put your shoes, belt, coat, hat and all earthly possessions into an x-ray tub, but you then have the opportunity to go into a lottery to determine if you get a full-body massage. This can involve a gentle wanding, a hands-on strip search and/or the possibility of a full-body x-ray suitable for framing. Some of the personnel are quite adept. One guy in Dallas was particularly friendly. I would, however, caution travelers to leave at home any body piercing jewelry that they might normally wear below the neck. I also don't think that money belts under the shirt would be a good idea. One other advisory here. I saw several people, including some security staff, require emergency medical assistance at a checkpoint in Chicago. It seems that a young college student had been required to remove his hiking boots, and his socks were emitting a purple gas. Wear clean socks and underwear when you travel. Your mother was right.

In general the flights ran on time and were relatively uneventful. The only cautionary warning I would give is that, whenever possible, you should travel with food from home. Once you go through the security gates, you are at the mercy of the terminal food services, and this is not good. The lines are long, the food service personnel have nicknames like "sleepy" and "dopey," and the passengers waiting in those lines seemed to possess a high potential for violence. Fortunately, security personnel had already noted this, and had forbidden the issuance of plastic knives to any customers.

Yes, there are some risks in traveling, but it can also be pretty entertaining. And, although the security personnel don't seem to have much of a sense of humor, the skies can still be really, really friendly. ◆

Revenge of the Pedestrian

INTELLECTUALLY CHALLENGED PEOPLE are literally driving me nuts. Everyone who knows me, understands what a patient, forgiving and tolerant person I am. Lately, however, despite my better instincts, I have been getting really torqued off by the sheer deluge of brain-disengaged, sensor-deficient, crash dummy-wannabes, who are on the roads this winter.

Yes, I am talking about you, or somebody you know, or maybe your kids, or their friends. Of course, I'm too nice a guy to actually come out and say that there are a lot of you out there who are stupid idiots, and who should never be allowed behind the wheel of a car, but sometimes I think it.

Let's talk about ice. Yes, I know, that's what you put in your drink to celebrate breaking the land speed record getting home from work. It's hard to match the satisfaction of chopping twenty-two seconds off your best winter time, and simultaneously teaching a couple of pedestrians, why they should be taking their chances on an unplowed, unsanded, pelvis-breaking sidewalk, rather than clogging up your personal speedway.

And don't worry about the fact that even 4000-pound vehicles don't have perfect traction on ice. After all, what's the sense in owning a four-by-four if you can't let everyone else eat ice chips. If someone is coming down a hill sideways, wearing a fright mask where his or her face used to be, don't get out of the way. No, instead, utilize the information that is being given you (that this could be one slippery hill). Rev your vehicle up to maximum speed, and go screaming right by them. You can make it up that sucker no matter what. And if you are planning on turning onto a side street halfway up the hill, make sure you cut the turn real fine so you can keep up your speed. And if you are the car coming to that intersection on the side street, make sure you get right out onto the hill, so that the other dumbo can see you at the last minute and go into his/her emergency, high speed, ice evasion tactics. Most of these involve lots of yelling and loud dissemination of new information about relatives, an occasional snow bank, and maybe the exchange of pertinent factual data, so that you can develop a long-term friendship.

And how about snow? Not the stuff like the White House drops on us everyday, and not the junk that some of you put up your nose, but the cold, white, slippery stuff that you drive on with mindless abandon. Did you ever think about not following right behind the plow/sander, especially on hills? Here's a surprise! These trucks are often driving on roads that haven't been plowed or sanded. Sometimes they need to back down the hills to regain momentum. Can you imagine that this could be a difficult maneuver if some mental moron is trailing along right behind them?

And how is your stopping ability on snow? Oh, that's right, you don't need your brakes because you have x-ray vision and can see what is behind all those snow banks. If you yell loud enough or really lean on your horn, that bozo who is slowly backing out of his driveway, between the high banks, will have enough sense to pull back in and get out of your way. And what parent in his or her right mind is going to let a small child out to play in the snow.

I know how precious time is to you. You need to spend at least five hours a day surfing the net, or making like a vegetable in front of the TV, and you certainly don't want to waste that valuable time on the roads. An hour on the turnpike at eighty mph will get you there fifteen or twenty minutes faster than doing the speed limit, so a super fast trip around town can probably save you one or two minutes a day. And every minute counts when you may be imbedded in a bridge abutment tomorrow.

So don't worry about your friends and neighbors who are scrambling for dear life on those roads. And, particularly if you drive a white Chevy Blazer, and nearly killed a guy and his dog out walking on Dwinell Drive last weekend, don't give it another thought. I'm sure that peanut-sized brain is too preoccupied with other, more important issues.

Just remember, however, that I know where you live. And although my dog may have had it all scared out of him that day, we're going to be making deliveries to your house regularly in the future. ◆

Playing Charity Golf

I BROUGHT MY GOLF CLUBS up from the basement this week. It's July and my golf season is about to begin.

I don't know why.

Every year I tell myself that I am not going to once again inflict upon my fragile psyche another season of pain and humiliation. But then these charity tournaments come along, and friends invite me to play in them. They do it so they can watch me make a fool of myself. This seems to give them pleasure.

I agree to this because I am a fine person who wants to help out some good causes . . . and because they usually have pretty good gift bags at these things. These gifts go to all participants, even me. The one problem with these little freebies is that most of them are golf-related, so I have to keep playing in order to use them. It's a vicious circle, which I can't seem to break.

Another attraction of these tournaments is that I almost never have to actually play my own horrible shots. As long as one person in the foursome hits a decent ball, everyone else can play from where he or she landed. This doesn't really cut down on my lost balls, but at least I don't have to spend as long looking for them.

I have noticed over the years that the "scramble" format has also encouraged other lousy golfers to stumble out onto the links. We are like a special fraternity of hackers. The golf pros at these courses would normally never let us near their precious tees and greens, but on this special day, they have no choice. And we pretty much tear the place up. We play from the wrong fairways, land on the wrong greens, bang balls off the roofs of the members' course-side homes, and generally scare the hell out of the real golfers. And it all can be classified as a noble effort to support needy charities.

I also find it really amusing that, occasionally, we win the good prizes. Over the years, I have won three special awards for sinking the longest putt on a designated hole. In one typical case (pre-scramble format), I was lying six or seven by the time I got to the green, and I was on the outer edge because I had just blown an easy chip. I then proceeded to sink a sixty or seventy foot putt to save my eight . . . and, oh yes, win the prize. One of the nice things about winning this prize is that it is a real advantage to be bad. The closer your approach shot lands to the pin, the less likely you are to be in position to sink the longest putt.

I have never understood, however, why they give a putter to the winner. I have three putters from these things, two of them beautiful handmade jobs that I wouldn't think of bringing on the course. Besides, my twenty year old Ping is the only thing in my bag that works. Why don't they give us something we can use, like a ball retriever or a three wood . . . or a lesson on getting out of the sand?

Even hackers like myself, however, eventually pick up a few pieces of useful golf wisdom from our years of appearances at these tournaments. And while they are not of much value to the good golfers out there, I think they could be useful to any of you who are actually thinking of following in my footsteps and playing in some of these tournaments.

Put your gift bag in the car before the tournament actually starts. That way they won't be able to confiscate it while you are still out on the course.

Be prepared for humiliation. You will always hit your worst shot when the most people are watching.

Golf balls are inherently cowards. They will invariably hide in the woods or tall grass in order to keep you from getting a clear shot at them. Water holes are a chance to exact your revenge on the ones that have performed the worst. Don't yell "die sucker" too loud, however, if people are putting on a nearby green.

The faster your swing, the more time you will have to look for your ball.

Always take the short cut over the trees when faced with a sharp dogleg. You're going in the woods anyway, so you might as well go out in style.

There will always be one guy in every foursome who points out that "it's still your turn," or "you didn't make it to the ladies' tee." Disposing of him, preferably early in the round, is the only appropriate reason to ever remove your 3 iron from your bag.

Don't waste your time figuring out if you have the right club for a particular shot. The chances of you hitting the ball properly are infinitesimal. And if you do hit it well, it will always be the wrong club. (This is humbly claimed as Currie's Law).

Bring lots of rain gear and pray for a downpour. This will be your only chance to actually win a tournament. We once finished second in an event in which they had to stop play and draw numbers to determine a winner. We were about a hundred over par at the time.

Never read any books on golf. They will only confuse you. Go out there without any plan except to have a few beers at the earliest opportunity.

Don't celebrate too wildly when you win the big raffle prizes at the post-tournament dinner. The real golfers all have bags full of potential weapons. ◆

The Ice Cream Man

THERE WAS A MAN on a three-wheel bike with a grindstone on the back, who came down our street a couple of times a year banging a gong, and all the housewives would bring their carving knives and scissors out to be sharpened.

Peddlers sold pots and pans off pushcarts, salesmen sold encyclopedias, vacuum cleaners and magazines door-to-door, and delivery men entered our homes carrying milk and bread.

And the ice cream man arrived on hot summer days, playing "Mary had a Little Lamb" or "London Bridges": a pied piper, with a trail of children carrying nickels and smiles.

In those days, it never occurred to us that the ice cream man could be evil. Or that the magazine salesman could be anything but what he seemed. The trust level was very high. People watched out for each other. And the system worked well.

Whether it was in naiveté or innocence, America thrived. And the integrity of neighborhoods was a critical part of the culture. We trick-or-treated without adult supervision and happily accepted all sorts of homemade offerings without worries of razor blades or drugs. People knew each other's names, or at least nicknames. Kids roamed free, using everyone's yards as a playground. They even organized their own games.

These neighborhoods started disappearing back in the 1960s. The peddlers were the first to go, then the salesmen and Avon ladies got caught in the changing dynamics of two-income families and archaic products. But we still retained a few last vestiges of the old communities. Magazine salesmen (college kids mostly) still came around, and kids doing fund-raisers. And we had new home delivery services, as fast food replaced home cooking. And, happily, we still had the ice cream man in his little truck with the delicious looking stickers pasted everywhere.

Then we heard the news that at least one ice cream man is alleged to be leading our children down different and scary paths, and the "college kids" were selling magazines to gain entrance to homes for burglary and rape. Recent incidents are even making the Girl Scouts have second thoughts about selling cookies door-to-door.

It is not a happy time for those of us who loved the open neighborhoods of our past. It is ironic that, in many communities, the homes are closer together but the neighbors are much further apart. People move in and out much more frequently and many aren't home during the day. Most are doing well if they know the last names of a few of the families living close by. Kids, roaming the area in groups, are viewed with suspicion. Owners are upset if kids wander through their yards, and doors are locked and often alarmed.

Neighborhoods that were once open environments for living and communicating and sharing life have been replaced by fortresses within which most of the conversations come from the questionable intellects of television talking heads.

The electronic media has added to the isolation by luring people indoors to enjoy the attractions of games and computers and cable TV. As part of that, they have made everyone much more aware of the evil out there. An incident in a small town in Nebraska is brought into the living room on the big screen, like it happened next door. Years ago, sitting on the back porch, playing Monopoly and listening to the crickets, we probably would have been blissfully ignorant of the event.

It is not surprising that we have developed wariness and cynicism into an art form in this country. And the activities of the "ice cream man" seem to have justified our growing trend towards family isolation. I wonder, however, if we aren't losing more than we gain by letting the hysteria of these incidents force us into continuing retreat from the world.

In the old neighborhoods, we learned from each other, and we developed an understanding and trust of each other that was, for the most part, rewarded. I know we can't bring that era back, but it would be a shame if we withdraw so totally from our environment that the only part of human nature that we see comes from the flickering screens of our TV sets, focusing on the sad sickness of those few who violate that trust. ◆

Backyard Vegetable Gardens

My wife suffers from a malady that seems to afflict many in New England. I believe the formal name for this illness is "wormabodus disruptus," but most know it by the more common descriptive term of "gardening." In particular, I refer to the deranged efforts by some of our citizens to grow backyard vegetable gardens.

I have never really understood the attraction of digging holes in the backyard. There seem to be better things that people could be doing with their spare time, like watching baseball games, playing golf or going to the beach. But every year, millions of amateurs go out to their backyards, armed with spades and trowels and bug spray and calamine lotion . . . and proceed to totally brutalize a good patch of earth. When we do this to another country, the world screams bloody murder, but if we do it out behind the garage, it is some kind of noble avocation.

I don't understand why these people don't leave the farming to the professionals. Real farmers know what they are doing and grow good stuff, like melons and sweet corn and beans. But backyard gardeners spend countless hours disrupting worms and grubs, so they can grow stuff like turnip, zucchini and gourds. What the heck do people do with gourds? Their only strong point is they will last for weeks, because no one eats them. And if zucchini is so good, how come every gardener in America spends most of the early fall trying to give the things away?

When I ask these questions of my wife, she tells me that working with the earth is a relaxing, healing process that counteracts the stresses of modern living. However, my unbiased observations of her work in the garden leave me skeptical of the whole process.

Let's look at a typical summer in the vegetable garden.

Dig up a patch of the yard, usually someplace where a horseshoe pit or barbecue should be.

Make a diagram for the garden that looks like the invasion plan for Normandy.

Wallow around in the dirt for hours at a time, fighting mosquitoes, black flies and snakes, in order to scientifically bury a bunch of plants and seeds; many of which will never look better than the day she puts them in the ground.

Build a fence around the garden to keep out all the little animals that want to eat the plants she just bought.

Get really upset and stressed out because those little animals are smarter than the average gardener, and find a way through the fence and eat all the little plants.

Buy new plants and build a bigger fence.

Buy fertilizer to spread on the plants. Fill the backyard with olfactory reminders of why we don't raise horses and opted for indoor plumbing.

Spend approximately two months pulling out all the stuff that really grows well in the garden, so the scrawny little plants can grow a little bigger.

Face the fact in late August or early September, that most of the "good stuff" in the garden isn't going to make it. But take solace in the fact that the zucchini is doing well.

Go to the farmers' market the next six weeks to buy all the good stuff that never made it.

Spend a month giving bags of zucchini to the neighbors, many of whom desperately flee when they see us approaching.

Give the sad remains of the garden a proper burial, after the first frost, and cover it with fertilizer and compost so there will be lots of disgusting stuff to dig up in the spring.

I never could figure out how this whole process actually reduced stress. She would spend all summer looking like a refugee from a mud slide and worrying about rain and sun and plant predators. The annual budget would include funds for plants, fertilizer, seeds, fencing material, equipment and gardening paraphernalia. I once estimated that the average cost of a tomato (counting her time at $8.00/hr) was about $143.00. Cucumbers probably cost about $18.00 each. Zucchini, of course, were cheap. But what do you really do with them? I know there are probably books out there telling you a thousand things you can do with a zucchini (and I can think of one more), but have you ever met anyone that looked forward to a big plate of the steaming stuff? My theory is that they're really weeds, but gardeners won't admit it.

There is no arguing with the bottom line, folks. You are much better off spending your summer hours watching bikinis at the beach, reading a book on the patio, or disrupting the plant and animal life at the golf course.

If you absolutely must spend your time communing with the worms and grubs, I suggest you stick with flower gardens, which are a whole lot cheaper and prettier. And if you get a few weeds in the flower garden, most of us won't know the difference. Some of them are prettier than the flowers. Weeds, like vegetables, are a matter of taste, but at least you don't have to eat the ones in a flower garden. ◆

Thayer Pond

THE TRAIL OF BUBBLES moved directly towards me, coming across the two acre pond at a jogger's pace. The water itself was dead calm . . . heavy from the weight of the leaves clogging its edges. Perhaps exhausted from bearing this burden, it radiated steam into the cool morning air.

I was standing by the overflow dam, mesmerized by the late fall scene. I leaned over to get a better view as the bubbles neared. Suddenly, not two feet from my nose, the head of an otter broke the surface and looked me right in the eye. I can still remember my surprise, which probably accurately reflected his fright at the unexpected meeting. As I jumped back, spilling my coffee and barely avoiding falling into Bow Brook, I could see his long body and tail desperately trying to catch up with the rest of him as he disappeared under the surface, never to be seen again.

This was my real introduction to Thayer Pond. When we had first looked at buying our home on the pond, I had been impressed with the gentle beauty of this little enclave, tucked away within a mile of the state capitol building. But I had also observed that the water had a rusty brown color that didn't give me much hope that anything really interesting lived in or around it. With my usual caution, I requested tests before purchasing the property to find out if pollutants might be a problem. The results showed traces of manganese and iron from the soil that caused the coloration, but also revealed that the water was reasonably clean.

The pond is a passthrough collecting spot for Bow Brook, which travels through much of the back country of northwestern Concord. It visits here briefly and departs over an old overflow dam that points it south to join the Merrimack River. The depth of the pond ranges from six inches to three or four feet right near the dam. Scattered among the shallows are tree stumps, the remains of a screen door, and an old wooden hockey goal left on the ice too long last winter. Countless other items probably rest on the murky bottom.

In the spring and summer, the area closes in tightly with heavy foliage. Children pull occasional small fish from the water, young lovers hide along the shore seeking privacy from the outside world, and high school kids, refugees from the school two blocks away, just plain hide.

The fall and winter are actually more interesting periods for the casual observer. The area opens up and the neighbors can see the pond more clearly. When the ice has firmed, children, and a few parents, come to skate and enjoy the atmosphere. When new snow falls, you can see cross-country skiers make their way across the pond and follow the brook. It is not unusual to see deer, in twos and threes, hesitantly pick their way along the edges, searching for food that has been grazed out further up country.

After my meeting with the otter, I realized there was a lot more going on here and I began to pay close attention to the changing culture of Thayer. I noticed the lone blue heron who was a frequent visitor throughout the summer. He would come early and wade in stealthy solitude in the shallow waters where the brook entered. He didn't like company and on those occasions when my presence was made known, he would run away across the water, spreading his huge angular wings and building speed until, almost miraculously, he became airborne, circling a couple of times to gain altitude and then disappearing north over the treetops.

For a brief two or three days when the ice first came in and went out, I also saw a single beaver appear, hovering over holes in the ice. I could never quite tell what he was doing, but he showed up at the same time for about five years and then was gone.

In late spring of our second year here, my oldest daughter and a friend decided to name the turtle inhabitants. They took the old canoe onto the pond, collected those residents who were slumbering in the sun and painted names on their shells with red nail polish. We were able to spot Bert and Ernie and Grover for a number of years thereafter as they made their ponderous journeys up the hill to lay eggs. I sometimes wondered what these indefatigable ladies felt about the selection of names.

The foxes came suddenly about three years later. Their presence was announced by the cacophonous chatter of the crows very early in the morning. If you got up immediately you could see them quietly crossing the yard, clearly angry at the noisy reception. Then one morning I went out the back door to open the garage and two of them were sitting on the rocks on the far side of the driveway. Neither the sound of the garage doors opening or the cars moving up and down the driveway seemed to disturb them. They stayed in a tall grassy area off the front yard for about two months and sunned themselves almost every day. Then one day they were gone as suddenly as they arrived.

Over recent years, the area has been visited by moose, a bear who launched a sneak attack on my neighbors beehives, the world's largest porcupine and an old VW Rabbit that mysteriously appeared one snowy Sunday morning in the brook about thirty yards below the dam.

Thayer Pond represents part of what I love about Concord and New Hampshire. There is something special about living in the shadow of the state capitol and still being so close to so much wildlife (especially since it isn't even an election year).

The blending of the environments of man and nature seems to work here, at least for the moment, and I plan to enjoy the opportunities it affords. It is the chance to stand by my window on an early winter morning and watch a pair of deer meander through the snow. And at lunch that same day hear the sounds of classical music drifting up from the pond as a solitary skater makes her graceful spins and jumps across the ice.

Perhaps one day I'll even see another trail of bubbles come to me across the water. ◆

Eva Cassidy's Message

I WAS DOWNTOWN the other day, trying to track down a CD by a performer for whom I had only half a name. As usual, Mike was able to sort out the mystery. But, knowing that I am always looking for interesting voices, he also asked me to listen to a couple of cuts from another album. And he told me the story of Eva Cassidy, a young woman whose life was cut short by melanoma at the age of 33.

It's hard to describe the emotions that I felt as I sat at home and quietly listened to her CD. Many of the songs were old standards. They were a mix of gospel, a little Irving Berlin, some folk and blues; actually the whole American musical experience seemed in some way to be wrapped up in it. And every song was a new one.

If I sound like I am contradicting myself, it's probably because I am. This young lady sang these songs in a way that made them different and unique to her. This pure voice, with a range the breadth of Oklahoma, traveled through me like a midnight train. Quiet vibrations, attention-getting power, a rush of emotions, and then a backflow breeze that left me with chills from my head to my heart. And as I listened, I was overwhelmed with what all of us had lost. As the recordings followed one after the other, her music seemed to speak for all those glorious, talented people in this world who have never had a chance to realize their potential. She seemed to sing for those whose voices and skills were lost to wars and disease and sometimes just bad luck: for John Seel and Dennis Barger and too many other friends from Dartmouth whose lives were cut short by Vietnam, and for Gary Dillon and Michael Briggs and all the other sons and daughters whose lives were never fully lived. People who might have filled our world with humor and friendship and perhaps great art or literature or medical miracles. Eva Cassidy's soul seemed to pour itself out in these songs, railing against the inequities and reaching for the heavens.

And as the album finally ended, soaring gently into silence, I could only feel an overwhelming sadness, because, in this case, I did indeed know what I had missed. This rare talent cut across all the false musical boundaries of race, religion, culture and style. And as I shut my eyes and listened to the beauty that flowed from "Over the Rainbow," I could hear her also singing for all those others, whose voices were silently passing with her over that rainbow. ◆

The Storm

I GOT A CALL THE OTHER DAY from an old friend. He had been laid off from his job. He was another casualty of the broad epidemic of downsizing that has been going on for several years.

Shortly after he lost his job, his wife, a fairly senior employee in a state agency, decided to divorce him because he was, in her words, a loser. He had then escaped to a consulting job in Spokane for a few months, but couldn't stand being away from his kids and had moved back to southern California.

When he called, he had no job, no wife, no assets and very little access to his kids. He had almost no hope. He had been dropped into that vast chasm that seems to have absorbed so many in recent years. A formerly successful individual suddenly becomes a non-person in our society. As I listened, I could feel the terror. I could envisage a man on a space walk who suddenly finds the umbilical cord to the ship severed. As he spins into the darkness, he sees a world of incredible beauty: a silent planet disappearing into the distance.

He had called me to find a little warmth and to see if I knew of any job opportunities. We talked of old friends, now scattered around the world, and of places to start over. I couldn't offer much real help, only sympathy and a couple of suggestions. We tried to fill the silences with a discussion of the weather. New Hampshire was in the middle of a major snowstorm combined with near zero temperatures. It was sunny and 73 in Newport Beach. He won a tiny victory in that exchange.

As I hung up the phone, I looked out the large floor-to-ceiling window in my study. The outside flood was on and I could see the snow dancing through the night. The flakes glinted like mica in the cold night air: sparkling chips from a black-granite sky, gleaming just out of reach and then disappearing into the night. The wind played with them, pushing them against the glass and then screaming in rage as it carried them away from the alien warmth.

By morning, about eighteen inches of snow had accumulated. A few flakes still drifted down but the storm was over. The trees, the land and the pond were all covered with a fresh white layer that made the world seem pristine. Plows were actively working the otherwise deserted streets. But then, as I watched, a lone man with a shovel came down the road. He stopped at two homes, trudging to the doors and then slowly making his way back to the street. To my consternation, he then began the long trek down my driveway. He was quite thin, unshaven and moved stiffly.

He rang the bell at the side door and when I answered he dispensed with any niceties and simply said, "Do you think you might want to have your walk or driveway shoveled?" I nervously, reflexively, declined. He said "thank you, anyway" and began the long walk back up the driveway.

It had caught me by surprise. I regretted that I hadn't even explained that I have a man contracted on an annual basis to plow the driveway. I also realized that he was the first shoveler I had seen out trying to make money after a storm in probably twenty years. Even the kids don't do it anymore. And then I thought about my friend and his struggles.

I also remembered the old car beside the garage that sometimes sits under snow for a week or two until I get around to digging it out. I chased him down as he was being turned away from another home up the hill. We agreed on ten dollars for him to shovel out the car and the breezeway.

I asked him what he did for a living. He was a house painter who was trying to make a little extra money to see him through a difficult winter. He said he hadn't had much luck.

When he had finished, I paid him and watched him walk to the top of the driveway, turn left, back towards town, and disappear. Shortly behind him came one of the big city plows, its yellow lights flashing a warning. It flipped snow and rocks and clumps of dirt into the building banks, clearing a path for the rest of the world to do its business. ◆

Getting Together for the Holidays

CHRISTMAS IS OVER, and we have survived. But, lately, it seems like every holiday is a close call.

Our family is getting older. The kids are married and in their late twenties, and while we are blessed to still have three of our parents who are able to share the holidays, they are also getting older and less mobile. The combination has made for some interesting celebrations.

Last year, for Thanksgiving, the kids could not make it back from Colorado and Texas, and my brother-in-law was convalescing with us after just having major back surgery. Nevertheless, we decided to get the rest of the family together. It resembled a Red Cross treatment center.

In the kitchen, my wife, cool and efficient on the outside, as she prepared a twenty-two pound turkey and sixteen different vegetables, was internally running on a treadmill as she tried to maintain order in the chaos that reigned throughout the house.

My dad was spending most of his day in the bathroom trying to deal with an elderly affliction that would eventually relieve itself in a way that sent our plumbing system to its knees, begging for mercy. My brother-in-law was spending his time flat on his back in the living room, sharing his misery with a changing audience of wheelchairs, walkers and canes, that were in almost constant motion as they sought entry to that major attraction, the only downstairs bathroom.

As the day moved along (at a walker's pace), my father, exuberant from his recent victory over our plumbing system, decided to walk without his walker, and tripped over our 110 year old (in dog years) dog. The poodle, who is also deaf and nearly blind, never saw it coming, and, as far as I can tell, never knew it happened. My father did a remarkably agile rolling fall, and emerged unscathed, except for some slight dizziness.

We then all sat down to a wonderful dinner filled with warm talk, remembrances and laughter. The events of the day were catching up with me quickly, however. And after getting everyone home about 4:30, I decided to make a quick visit to the Emergency Room to see if I should be concerned about the heart palpitations that started hitting around the time of dad's fall. After several hours of tests and observation, it was determined that I was simply suffering from (surprise) stress.

Susanne, meanwhile, had managed to get her brother back upstairs to bed and we ended the day burying the stress under turkey sandwiches.

This year we decided to take a pass on a family get together for Thanksgiving, because the kids were still away and we had learned that we needed younger recruits to successfully handle a holiday. We decided to wait until Christmas, when my younger daughter and her husband would be with us. We knew this would still be fraught with some risk since I would be a pre-existing casualty for the season with recently completed bilateral hernia surgery, and would be even more useless than usual. But with extra young people around, the feeling was: how hard could it be? For the record, I was still on painkillers at the time and cannot be held responsible for any participation in this decision.

The omens were not good, however, as our brand new washing machine conked out the day of the arrival of our houseguests. And let me state that although the Maytag man may be sitting by the phone collecting cobwebs, there is apparently a two week wait to get a Whirlpool repairman to make a visit.

Despite this, however, Susanne, an expert in strategic planning, had sufficient clean laundry to see us through and she cooked the meal a day ahead of time. We felt ready to just focus on each other and enjoy Christmas Day.

Things started going wrong almost immediately. My mother-in-law's wheelchair went missing from her room at the assisted living center and we had to borrow a different larger one which proved very difficult to get up the stairs to our house. The result was a lot of heavy lifting (but not by me). Then minor disaster struck. My daughter and son-in-law were picking up my folks, and while Craig was bending and twisting over my dad to buckle his seat belt, he popped out his back, which had probably been previously stressed working on the wheelchair. Craig, who is six feet four, then rode in the back of the Saab back to the house. It took a half-hour to get him out of the car. And we had to use farm implements (an edger and a hoe) as makeshift canes to get him into the house.

Fortunately, once in the house, we remembered that we happened to have an extra walker in the basement. (Doesn't everyone?) This brought the vehicle count in the house to two walkers, a wheelchair (and a cane). I could go with this and write a new Christmas carol but I'll spare you.

My brother-in-law soon arrived, still nursing a bad back after a year, and was able to provide Craig with lots of sympathy and advice.

The rest of the day went relatively well. There were a few minor collisions between walkers and wheelchairs, and the dog fell down the stairs once, but generally, it was quiet. The plumbing worked, everyone enjoyed their presents, and my father and I played Christmas carols before we all sat down to a masterful pre-cooked turkey dinner.

My daughter and wife, the only two remaining able-bodied residents (women always seem to be the survivors), were able to get my mother-in-law in her wheelchair back out to the car successfully. Then my daughter took her husband to the Emergency Room where Craig was able to get some pills that made him pretty happy.

In retrospect, despite the fact that ER visits seem to be becoming a family tradition, and the whole day played out against a backdrop of terrorist threats and mad cow disease, we all felt pretty fortunate.

We had survived another holiday, and in reality we were very grateful. We had been able to get together with most of our family, and we were able to keep our sense of humor and laugh off the minor problems, rather than crying over major ones. And it truly is a joyous time of the year for Christians. A day of warmth and remembrance and hope for the future. And I pray that we will have the opportunity for many more such holidays.

My only request is that next time, we demand that my older daughter and her husband also be in attendance. Clearly, we need a few more able-bodied reinforcements around for our kind of rowdy celebration. ◆

Bathroom Etiquette

MOST OF US IN NEW HAMPSHIRE probably consider ourselves to be reasonably civilized. In large parts of the state we have running water, refrigerators and cool electronic equipment like color TVs. We also have progressed to the point where we use napkins instead of our sleeves at dinner, and usually don't settle border disputes with firearms.

There is one area, however, where personal observation leads me to believe that men need a lot of work. That is the subject of proper bathroom behavior. I don't know whether this is because some of us have just emerged from the outhouse era, or we just haven't yet learned all of the blessings of running water and flushable toilets.

For whatever reasons, it seems an appropriate time to provide a brief set of guidelines for acceptable bathroom etiquette.

The toilets in most modern bathrooms actually do flush. It is not dangerous to push the little lever or button after you have done your business. (Unless you are using a gas station toilet or the facilities at a Red Sox game, where you may need to use common sense.) Yes, I know it can also be confusing when you come across a toilet that automatically flushes. In that case, try this rule. If it doesn't automatically flush, look for a little lever or button.

Wash your hands after use. Studies show that a depressingly large number of our residents have a tough time with faucets and sinks. If these intimidate you, practice at home, so you're not embarrassed in public. Then when you are in a restroom, get all your brain cells pulling together, and try working through the complexities of soap and water.

Try your best to discard the toilet paper in the toilet bowl and the paper towels in the trash. I know this is complicated and many of you are lousy shots, but . . . That reminds me, it is a well-known fact that most men can't hit the side of a barn when they are doing their business. So why do some restaurants put newspapers above the urinals? Are they crazy? Think about it. Old guys are notoriously poor shots. Now imagine them trying to put on their glasses to read a newspaper while operating runaway equipment.

Please ensure that you leave all toilet paper in the bathroom. Do not carry an emergency supply on your shoe, or elsewhere. I once saw a guy walk around a store for fifteen minutes and then walk out the door trailing a four foot strip of paper from the back of his belt. It is not a good image.

I am sure that with a little hard work, all of us can some day master these difficult concepts. And I can testify that the alternative isn't good. I was down in Massachusetts recently, and they are so backward down there, that some places actually have live attendants in some of the restrooms just to make sure you do it right. And then they want you to give them money. ◆

Leaders of the Free World

DID YOU EVER WONDER how we got to be the "leader" of the free world? It is hard to believe that it is the result of the quality of our politicians.

Most of our leaders seem to be in Washington because their other careers went dead, or maybe they never had another career. And a lot of them aren't able to apply themselves well at this job either, based on the amount of time they actually spend representing us at the various legislative meetings.

But once elected, they don't appear to have much to worry about, because our voters don't seem to care. Apparently our voters are so dumb they can't even figure out a butterfly ballot, let alone determine if their representative is earning his paycheck.

No wonder the rest of the world is a little worried about us. Our election standards are even lower than our education standards.

Right now, any idiot who is a natural-born citizen and is at least thirty-five years of age, can run for President. And a lot of them have taken advantage of that opportunity. The election process isn't doing a very good job of culling the herd. We, as voters, keep putting people into office and then complaining that they are in office. Then we nominate an even bigger idiot to try to replace him or her.

I think, as keepers of the first real primary, we have some responsibility to ourselves and the world, to establish a few minimum requirements to be eligible to be a leader of the free world. And maybe we should also impose a few demands on our voters as well.

For our would-be presidential candidates, I suggest the following eligibility standards:

Live in an apartment without a doorman for at least a year.

Serve at least one year in any combination of the following non-supervisory jobs: food service, manufacturing, sales, health care, transportation, construction, or education.

Complete two years of service in the military, the Peace Corps or an equivalent (without a valet or PR person to assist).

Ride a public bus across country, stay at least one night in a flop house, and spend at least two weeks in a place without indoor plumbing.

Demonstrate the ability to successfully run an organization that is not inherited or funded by family trusts.

Personally fill out and file a federal tax return.

Demonstrate a sense of humor and the common sense to recognize BS when it is up to the ankles.

Read at least one trashy novel and watch a week of daytime television.

Demonstrate a working knowledge of baseball and football.

Spend a month as a teacher's aide in an inner city public school.

As for the voters, my expectations must be much more limited. But even with that realization, it seems that there should be a few basic requirements, none of which are currently being enforced. Voters should be expected to do the following:

Prove they are United States citizens.

Only be allowed to vote once in each election.

Be required to identify themselves at the polls. (If they don't know who they are, they probably shouldn't be voting.)

Be declared ineligible if they are convicts or persons legally rendered incompetent.

Be a human being. (No more dogs or parrots getting the vote).

Have a pulse.

Be able to state the last name of the person for whom Washington, D.C. was named.

None of the above requirements are particularly demanding for either the voters or the future leader of the free world. They might, however, go a long way towards ensuring the humanity of those involved in the election process. ◆

C-C-Christmas Commercials Are Over

As I bask in the joyful feeling of the holidays . . . being over, I have a sense of spiritual renewal. Once again, it feels safe to watch the mindless stuff that TV spits out to me on a regular basis. I have survived another year of Christmas commercials.

I have come to believe that the onerous burden of these things is basically a factor of cumulative impact and is therefore significantly less a risk for the young. As one who slightly predates the birth of commercial television, however, I have endured several generations of Christmas commercials and can comment authoritatively that the long-term impact is bad for your mental health. In my early years, I would get a little nauseated after the fifty-second viewing of a typically bad ad from Hamilton blender, but I could live through it with some degree of equanimity. I had stamina. I had been through a three-month ballroom dancing class with Mrs. Hess. I felt I could handle anything.

As the years passed, however, it became apparent that the holiday ads weren't going to go away and that no matter what my physical and mental conditioning, I was ultimately going to be overwhelmed by the sheer volume and inanity of the onslaught. And every year the advertising industry started a little earlier and attacked a little more aggressively. They also refined their techniques so that there was almost no hope in avoiding being turned into a mindless, moving MasterCard.

I have tried a few defenses which did show temporary success. The most useful was to immerse myself in football. I found that if I watched several hours of these games, my mind turned to fuzz, and I became partially inoculated to the ads. I think of this as the Chris Schenkel defense. A mind can only absorb so many stupid statements in any defined period of time. Once you have reached your limit, everything else just kind of rolls off you. For me, two football games in a six hour period could protect me from Obsession commercials for up to two days. This still left many unprotected days, however, and six or seven weeks of promos for things like Roger Whitaker's Christmas CD could really take its toll. Nothing can protect your sanity when assaulted with a steady barrage of "Holly Jolly Christmas."

It is, however, the realization that some of these commercials will be coming back forever, that causes me to slip into my ultimate, glazed-eye, semi-comatose defense. This usually occurs about a week before Christmas and sometimes lasts until the new year. My wife hates this one because it sometimes involves a lot of drooling and quite a bit of beer.

Let me give you some examples of the ads that can bring on immediate entrance into this near-vegetative state:

1) Ch-Ch-Ch-Chia pets. And now they have Chia heads. For those of you in another galaxy, these are pieces of pottery, shaped like animals and peoples' heads. They have some kind of vegetation growing out of them. An announcer with the most annoying voice in broadcasting history, does the ads. (Okay, maybe he's second to Kerry Strugs.)

These are only sold at Christmas, because no human on the planet would be stupid enough to buy one for himself. I can only imagine for whom people buy these things. Perhaps someone still in mourning over the death of their pet rock.

2) White Diamond perfume, as advertised by Liz Taylor. Liz, in all her abundant splendor, takes a large bauble off her ear and throws it into the middle of a poker game saying, "These have always brought me luck." The implication is that she is bailing out some loser who has finally gotten a good hand but doesn't have enough money to play.

What this has to do with perfume is beyond me, but the idea that Liz is going to make us all non-losers, is a little hard to swallow (or smell). This is a lady who has spent the last thirty years in alcohol and drug rehab, and has had eight (?) marriages. That probably means at least six divorces, not counting repeats. That certainly explains the rehabs, but I'm not sure I want her, or someone who smells like her, backing my efforts at the poker table, or anywhere else. Amazingly, this ad has been running for several years, so someone is actually buying this stuff.

3) CK Be perfume. Black and white pictures of emaciated children. This is apparently a perfume for men and women. Presumably because we all want to smell alike. That is certainly what I've been looking for. All of the kids in these ads look like they are refugees from Bosnia. Some of them have shirts on and some don't, but it's impossible to tell male from female. There are lots of big, hollow eyes, and nobody looks like they have ever been happy. This is the gift that the new boyfriend with the nose ring and dressed in "rapper threads" will be sharing with your fifteen-year-old daughter.

4) Ginzu knives. I'm not sure I'm spelling this right because all I can remember are whirling knife blades. They're the ones that cut anything. The ads show a chef cutting and dicing everything in the kitchen, and

then shows the same knife being used to cut through twenty-seven kinds of metal and plastic. This is clearly the perfect gift for anyone wishing to recut a section of sewer pipe and then come upstairs and carve the holiday turkey.

I shouldn't really be rehashing these things, however, since we are now safe from Christmas ads for another six or seven months. It is, instead, a time for rejoicing in the new year and reactivating my few remaining brain cells . . . which I plan to attempt right after the Super Bowl. ◆

Winter Insanity

Down south they love to show pictures of the winter storms that assault those of us who live in New England. They know it's good for the tourist business, and it also reinforces their notion that most of us are crazy.

After three months of weather like we have had this year, there may be more than a little substance to the insanity charges. All you have to do is look at some of the video of recent storms, and you can see ample cause for thinking that people might be on the verge of some kind of breakdown.

I see tortured souls with glazed eyes peeking over head-high snow banks, and cars upside down on median strips. There are pictures of snow-clogged roads where you need Lojack to find the car you parked the previous night, and icicles precariously hanging over entrances, promising instant death to the unwary. And let's not forget the bursting pipes causing picturesque frozen waterfalls down the sides of unsuspecting homes.

Even in ordinary times it is hard to refute that at least some of us may be a few shingles short in the roof department.

One clear example is the image that many of us project by the clothes we wear. Sure, we feel we are being practical, but to the outside world we conjure up visions of Johnny Carson in red plaid. Headgear is the most visible part of our winter dress and sends a powerful message to others. The mix of psychedelic ski hats, earflap caps, mufflers, face masks and ear muffs (sometimes in combination), makes us look like a bunch of hicks (and yes, I am aware that is the look that many of us are going for). When this is combined, however, with the multi-layered, double-wide, coat look, we have a presentation that causes others to speculate about our sanity. I even wonder myself sometimes, since I have heard of people slipping on the ice and lying there for hours because their hands can't reach the ground and their head is too muffled up to yell for help.

And then there is the general skepticism with which much of the world views our choices of exotic winter sports. Let's analyze why some might say we are crazy for participating in some of these.

Snowmobiling. Think about this. Bikers (perhaps not the most solidly-grounded group to begin with) put away their big hogs for the winter because they figured out, probably after years of study, that riding around in 10 degrees below zero wind chill isn't the most fun in the world. But some of our citizens love nothing better than to jump on snowmobiles, stare frostbite in the face, and head out across frozen lakes, where they risk becoming submersible popsicles. The ultimate pleasure for them, I am told, is to race these noisy vehicles into the wilderness, where they can enjoy the quiet beauty of a winter wonderland.

Ski Jumping. Here is a sport where the objective is to go downhill as fast as you can in order to launch oneself off a take-off pad that sends you flying off the mountain. You then try to execute a controlled crash a few hundred feet below so that you don't kill yourself.

Snowboarding. This appears to be a combination of downhill skiing and demolition derby. Participants get out on the side of a mountain, strap a board to their feet, and then slide down the mountain while dodging trees, skiers, and other snowboarders, most of whom are fifteen-year-old kids. These are kids who have not yet learned fear, relish being out of control, and will not be eligible to drive a car for another year; at which point, they will become the most dangerous people on the highways.

Polar Bear Clubs. This is supposedly a sport. It consists of screaming, near-naked people who run across the snow in the middle of the winter, dive into ice cold water, jump around for a couple of minutes turning blue, and then drive to the nearest hospital.

Snowshoeing. Participants in this growing sport snap on a pair of clown shoes, and then go wandering in the deep snow into the most inaccessible parts of the forest. This is only good news to the hungry carnivores who live there and like warm-blooded mammals who are slow afoot.

Ice Fishing. This sport involves sitting in a smoke-filled wooden hut, huddling around a hole in the ice and waiting to freeze to death. Once in a while an unsuspecting fish will be caught because the poor fish couldn't imagine anyone being stupid enough to sit out on a frozen lake all day holding a long string.

I could go on but I think you may be getting my point. The message we are sending to the rest of the country could be misinterpreted and lead to the conclusion that we are all idiots.

Now some of you are probably smiling and thinking that you would never get tarnished with those accusations because you go to Florida in the winter. This is not necessarily an indicator of superior intelligence and doesn't really help our reputation. Let's analyze Florida for a minute. This is a flat, hot place covered with swamps, parking lots and golf courses. The average age is 106, and it is the only place in the world where the sixteen-year-old driver is in a low risk insurance category. No one uses the beaches, it is suggested that golfers wear helmets, and the only time people smile is when the six o'clock news shows the latest New England blizzard.

The single valid reason a person would go to Florida is to watch spring training, which only occurs in March. The rest of the year, a trip to Florida is almost prima facie evidence that the winter has indeed made you crazy. You say you are going there to see Mickey Mouse? Think about that for a moment. You are hopping on a plane and flying 2000 miles to see a fake mouse. That will certainly convince the skeptics.

I guess you can see why some people get the wrong impression about us. They don't understand that all of this is just a way of blowing off a little steam as we enjoy the challenges and rewards of being hardy New England residents.

I know that, personally, I find these long winters very relaxing. They give me the chance to appreciate the beauty of the changing seasons and to be a little more introspective. And I have found a winter sport that makes a lot more sense than the craziness that attracts some of you. I have become a major participant in the art of indoor bike riding. I just hop on my stationary bike and log in the miles. This gives me all the exercise of riding a real bike, and I don't have to go anywhere. I can just pedal and pedal . . . and look out the window at the snow . . . and I'm still right here . . . looking at the snow . . . and pedaling . . . ◆

Looking Past Our Winter of Discontent

HAVE YOU NOTICED that we got what we asked for this winter? Yes, we brought this on ourselves.

Last fall, a number of you geniuses complained about smelly water in the Concord system. From those complaints, which were vociferous enough to be the subject of an article in the *Monitor*, it was a short trip to having the Concord hydrologists blaming it on the lack of snow. Supposedly, we needed a heavy and long snow cover on our reservoir to block out the sunlight and kill all that nasty algae that made our water taste like it had been filtered through Dennis Rodman's old sweat socks.

Well, I hope you are happy. There are parts of my driveway that I haven't seen in months, and my dog has been doing his business in the same sixteen square foot section of my backyard for so long that grass won't grow there again until the next millennium. (He's a small dog, he only goes in a shoveled area, and my wife refuses to shovel a bigger area).

I would guess that right about now any of those little algae guys that are still around are begging for mercy. I know I am. And I've noticed that my water definitely smells and tastes better. Despite that, I find myself drinking mostly bottled water. There is something about drinking dead algae that makes me pause before I refresh.

This article is not about complaining, however. I am basically a positive person, and I am looking past my plow, sanding and loader bills, and this long, cold, relentless, ice-encrusted, road-clogging, depression-inducing, energy-draining, white monster of a winter.

Instead, I have entered that stage of the seasons where delusion has once again overcome reality, and I am able to look forward to spring with a total lack of perspective.

I can actually envision myself playing golf again. Last fall, I solemnly swore that I would never again endanger mammal, bird, fish and plant life with my presence on a golf course. Now, I'm thinking that new clubs might fix my problems. Hey, they didn't officially ban me from Beaver Meadow; they just always seemed to have closed the course when I came to play.

I am seriously thinking about joining the Appalachian Mountain Club and breathing the fresh air at the top of the Presidential Range. (This may take a little conditioning work, since I currently get out of breath putting on my snow boots.)

I am actively planning a return to the beach despite the threat of UV rays. I realize this could be bad for me, and probably bad for anyone watching, since I have spent all winter eating my way out of depression. But what the heck, I'm hearing the Sirens' song of warm summer breezes and children building sand castles. As long as the "Save the Whales" groups don't come along, roll me onto a rubber mat and float me back out to sea; it will be worth the embarrassment.

Basically, I am bringing a message of hope. When things seem darkest, the thing that separates those of us who survive in New Hampshire from ordinary individuals is that we can persevere. And the way to do this is to ignore reality. We can imagine spring flowers, birds singing, hair regrowing, free parking, courteous drivers, no new taxes, and a land full of love.

I am here to tell you to follow those dreams, take the road less traveled, (even if it hasn't been plowed), and "don't stop thinking about tomorrow." But be careful about drinking the water. I hear it can make you delusional. ◆

The Chump in "Schlump"

WHEN I WAS A STUDENT at Dartmouth about a million years ago, we used to call the early spring mud season "schlump." It just sounded appropriate to the period. It was that time of year when everything was mud and melting snow and you needed wooden boards on the walkways to cross the Green. For most of us at the college and I dare say in New Hampshire, it was not a popular period. The only bright spot was that we knew spring couldn't be too far behind.

A week or so ago, in a burst of optimism and in desperation to get outside after another spring snowstorm, I convinced my skeptical wife to go for a walk with me and enjoy the emerging sunshine. We dodged the mounds of snow and the slush and headed for a nice little sandwich place near the high school.

The temperature was in the 60s. I was rapidly convincing myself that in a couple of more days the snow would be gone and I'd be hitting fungoes to my daughters at the ball field.

We headed up a well-traveled road next to the high school. I noticed quite a few students taking what I was sure was a well-earned break from classes. They were sitting on the steps or standing in the bright sunshine. As we walked, I closed my eyes, lifting my face to the heavens in thanks for this beautiful day.

Into this idyllic scene came the Toyota from hell. The driver must have revved the engines at the light because she had the car doing about forty within sixty yards of the intersection and was still accelerating rapidly. Susanne, who is much smarter than I am, bailed out to a snow-covered sidewalk. In my foolish reverie, I was still wandering along the edge of the road when the Toyota hit the slush and the mud-filled pothole.

The result was a perfect wave. Since I had forgotten my surfboard, however, I could only passively appreciate the symmetry of the moment. Ice, water and mud covered me. It was down my collar, in my ear and up my pants legs.

As I turned to watch the Toyota speed on, I could hear the cheers rise from the audience at the school. I realized that these kids were a tough crowd and that to elicit cheers from such a jaded group must have taken a spectacular performance. Through slush-covered eyes, I stood and contemplated the only written message declared by the Toyota as it disappeared toward town. The rear bumper had a sticker that read "I brake for Moose."

As I removed the layers of pre-spring from my body, I tried to understand the bumper sticker's meaning. What was it really saying? You would have to be an idiot to take it at face value. I mean who but someone that is certifiable is not going to brake for moose. Moose are big. Moose are not too smart. Moose are not predictable. If you run into a moose in your car, you are probably going to total your vehicle and very likely kill yourself.

Of course the message could also be to let the moose know which cars would stop for them if they decided to take a stroll on the highway. Stupid as moose are, however, I think even they know that anybody who sees a moose standing in the road is going to try to avoid it, and that putting on the brakes is a good first step.

Then it dawned on me that the message wasn't really about braking for moose at all. As my youngest daughter would say, "Duh." For those without teenagers that translates to: "You're a little slow on the uptake, aren't you, Dad?" Anyway, I realized that what the driver was saying was: I brake *only* for moose. Anything smaller on the road had better watch out.

Except right after Thanksgiving dinner, I am smaller than a moose, thus I guess I was fairly warned. Of course the driver hadn't put the warning on the front bumper where it would have given me a chance to react. In fact, this is almost universally a back bumper message—maybe to tell you why you have just been slimed or otherwise incapacitated.

As we continued what was a very soggy walk to the restaurant, I felt slightly better for having clarified this mystery. After all, spring was in the air, schlump could only last a couple of more months, the students at the high school had gotten a little free entertainment, and somewhere, the owner of a red Toyota was painting another pedestrian insignia on her door. ◆

Solution to Global Warming

I'VE BEEN DOING SOME THINKING about global warming. All the recent publicity about its dangers has gotten me seriously concerned. We have testimony about the threat, not only from Al Gore, but from other nationally recognized figures like Charlie Sheen, Paris Hilton and Rosie O'Donnell. It is clearly a real problem.

Initially, I was led to believe that the cause was a bunch of unthinking folks driving big SUV's, and maybe those politicians in Washington emitting all that hot air. But, recently, I read an article that stated that the biggest contributors to our ozone hole are cows. Yep, old Bessie's flatulence is what is really doing us in.

When I looked at the big picture, this made a lot of sense. While I personally didn't think Bessie's little issues were that bad, I had long sensed that it was a problem being downwind from Vermont.

As I pondered the Earth-destroying subject of cow flatulence, it suddenly came to me that this could be the solution to many of New Hampshire's problems. We could seize the opportunity to be on the cutting edge of this issue. Why not sell "flatulence credits"? Al Gore has been extremely successful with his company that sells "carbon credits."

We could copyright flatulence credits and then sell them to cow owners. This would in turn let them off the hook on global warming. They could put little stickers on their milk and cheese and butter certifying that they are "flatulence friendly."

The concept would work like this, initially. The state sells these credits to cow owners and in return agrees to remove one can of beans from New Hampshire store shelves for each cow credited. Ultimately, of course we would license this worldwide and collect a fee for every credit sold. We would in turn use the revenue from the credits to pay for schools and other needs, and maybe build some giant wind-power fans at the Vermont border to blow Vermont's flatulence down to Massachusetts, where they are used to bad odors.

This would solve a lot of global warming problems. Cow flatulence would be offset by a reduction in human flatulence, our taxes would probably go down, and we would be drinking environmentally-approved dairy products. The only losers would be the growers and processors of beans. But I have a solution to that also. We just get Congress to pass a bill requiring all vehicles to start using a new fuel blend called beanahol. Then everyone would be a winner.

Who knows, once drivers got a good whiff of the beanahol emissions, we might see a lot fewer drivers on the road. This might solve the global warming problem completely, and New Hampshire could take its rightful place as the state that let the air out of the flatulence balloon. ◆

There Oughta Be a Law, Oh Wait, There Is One!

WE HAVE TOO MANY LAWS! Every time some politician or pressure groupie wakes up with a bad hair day, Congress or some state or city governing body passes a new statute. This has been going on since 1776 and is an accelerating trend. We keep adding new laws and hardly ever take the old ones off the books.

The lawyers like to joke that we are no longer the "land of the free" but instead are the "land of the fee," and they are right. Before we say or do almost anything in the current litigious atmosphere, we need to check with a lawyer, accountant, environmental consultant, or OSHA expert, to make sure we aren't breaking some kind of statute or code. And a lot of times you can't even get a straight answer from them, because so many laws are vaguely written or archaic. Some of these laws are so old and out of touch with present society that they haven't been enforced in years. But they are still there and are available to be pulled out at a moment's notice, to be used by angry enforcement personnel for selective prosecution.

The Supreme Court recently addressed this when they tossed out the selective prosecution of someone for a bedroom law which had been on the books for years, but was almost never enforced. There are similar laws out there for a whole range of "crimes against the state," including a slew of other bedroom violations, safety regulations, dress codes, and general "busybody" intrusions.

I started to wonder how many of these laws I might have violated at one time or another. I decided to think about a normal event that might have turned me into a criminal somewhere in this country. I thought about my morning walk. Correct that, a hypothetical walk that I might have taken but really never did. Here is a list of hypothetical actions that would have gotten me in trouble somewhere in the United States, although not necessarily in Concord.

- I jay walked across several side streets.
- I walked on the grass in Capital Park.
- I loitered outside the bagel shop.
- I littered by tossing some bagel bits to the birds.
- I actually did feed the birds (two sparrows).
- I cussed at a car that almost ran me over in the crosswalk.
- I used a handicapped stall in the McDonalds men's room (they only have one stall).
- I wore a Dartmouth Indian t-shirt.

I also observed the following crimes being committed:

- A really heavy guy jogged by me topless.
- A kid was riding his bike on the sidewalk.
- A lady was walking her dog and he was not on his leash.
- A dog did publicly defecate in Bicentennial Square (without bag).
- A guy publicly grabbed his girlfriend's rear end.
- A lady plugged a meter.
- A guy popped his four-year-old on the bottom after the kid ran out into the street.
- A motorcycle couple drove down Main Street without helmets.

Now I know many of you are saying that I am ridiculous for even bringing this stuff up, but somewhere in this country there are groups of people who are horrified by each of these actions, and are ready to prosecute. Actually, if they saw it, everyone would be ready to prosecute the topless guy.

The thing that really scares me, however, is that not only do we have a lot of dumb laws on the books, but also we keep putting out new ones every day. And no one seems to sunset any of them.

We could easily have laws soon for all sorts of things from banning fast foods, to demanding the wearing of sunglasses in sunny climates, to requiring restrictor plates on cars. There is no end in sight to the foolishness of some of this stuff.

So the next time you take a walk, or work in your garden (poppies may soon be illegal), or build a deck with pressure-treated wood, or go to Burger King, get some legal advice, or face the possibility of spending a few years in the slammer.

As the keeper of the flame for "living free," New Hampshire needs to take a stand and tell all the nanny's to take a seat. ◆

Getting Ready for the Beach

I HAVE SPENT PARTS of the last thirty years at York Beach, Maine (sometimes also known as Concordville because so many Concord residents vacation there). It is a great place to go for a change of pace. I like the sounds of the ocean, the cool sea breezes, the excitement and activity of the area, and the ever-changing scenery (both on the water and the sand). For years, however, I have been trying to figure out what motivates individuals to spend all those hours actually lying on the beach. I couldn't understand why theoretically normal and sane people would find pleasure in oiling themselves up, and then alternately frying themselves in the hot sand and freezing in the numbingly cold waters of the North Atlantic. I was unsuccessful in obtaining a government grant to pursue an analysis of this (apparently they were already over budget for these kinds of projects). I decided, however, to continue with research on my own, as a service to my fellow man.

After years of study, and many long hours with the binoculars, I believe I have been able to classify, in general terms, some of those who seem so addicted to blistered skin, sand in intimate places, and heart-stopping, cold water baths. I thought it might be useful to share some of the results of this research with you prior to the arrival of the new beach season. This might allow you to better evaluate the situation if you, a normal person, were to suddenly find yourself surrounded by a broad cross-section of certifiable crazies at such a beach.

The following categories comprise the major groups of beach dwellers. They are listed in no particular order:

1) *Polar Bears*. There are people out there who actually like to swim in freezing water. Some of them can be seen on TV in the winter, diving into holes in the ice. This is part of their training program so that the York Beach water doesn't seem too cold. I suspect that their brains were fried in a previous summer's heat, and now they have the uncanny ability to actually thrive in water that makes the rest of us turn blue. Most of these people have been preparing for years for this test, their bodies are well-oiled, and the tide tends to rise when they go in.

2) *Max-Tanners*. These are people who use the beach to release their inhibitions. Many of them wouldn't be caught dead in a revealing blouse on Main Street, but will basically strip down to their underwear as soon as they are standing on sand. The theoretical rationale is that this is the only way they can get a really good tan. The actual objectives vary, from impressing boyfriends or girlfriends, to enjoying the sense of freedom and release that comes from running around nearly naked. There is a kind of selective amnesia related to this, and that is probably a good thing. It definitely adds life to the beach scene but can be a real mixed blessing. There are some cases where there is more to meet the eye than the eye is ready for.

3) *Voyeurs*. Many beach-goers fall into this category. They come to see everyone else. Unfortunately beach etiquette demands that they also wear bathing suits. This can be particularly unpleasant. One ameliorating factor with this group is that they burn easily and therefore often cover up fairly quickly. They also tend to have very short attention spans, except when confronted with world-class max-tanners. Since York Beach is not Malibu, they often get bored and hot, and wander into town to buy ice cream and add to their collection of ugly t-shirts.

4) *Perpetual Motion Machines*. A wide variety of kids add excitement and diversity to the beach scene. These youngsters have been resting up all year for beach day. They are impervious to cold water, are quite good at warming up tidal pools, love to splash those who wander too close to the ocean, and kick sand in food and drinks as they run over bodies

and drip on towels. They are relentless in their activities, never sleep and have great lungs, which help maintain a decibel level that appears essential to maintaining the chemistry of the beach.

5) *Beasts of Burden*. These are mostly out-of-shape fathers who are on an involuntary conditioning program. They don't actually spend much time on the beach, but they can be seen making frequent trips between car or cabin and the established beachhead. They carry inner tubes, folding chairs, shovels, pails, towels, big hats, cushions, binoculars, beach umbrellas, radios, wagons, strollers, blankets and a wide assortment of toys. The kids mostly ignore this stuff and the mother generally is too busy to use it, but it definitely contributes color to the setting. Most of these trips are scheduled at the hottest part of the day.

6) *Unofficial Assistant Lifeguard*. There are always a few of these guys on the beach. They roam back and forth looking for their lost youth. They can be identified by the tiny little bathing suits that they wear, and the tendency to have more hair on their backs than on their heads.

7) *Mummified Remains*. These are veteran beach goers who were left out in the sun too long, and are now a permanent part of the landscape. They are there when you get there, and they are there when you leave. They never seem to move, and probably own that piece of beach by virtue of squatter's rights. With luck, they will wake up before the guys with the metal detectors come by and try to grab their earrings and keys.

I hope that this summary of my years of beach study will be useful to you in understanding the dynamics of this primitive culture. Obviously, most of you do not fall into any of these categories, but are, instead, just normal, healthy people looking to get away from the hot weather. And if you are also interested in doing scientific studies of beach culture, York Beach is a pretty good place to start. ◆

Antiquing

THE FIRST THING YOU NEED TO KNOW about antiquing is that those of us who do it are crazy. There is no other way to describe people who get up at 5:00 a.m. on weekends, drive sometimes hundreds of miles, and run around open fields in all kinds of weather looking for what any sane person would define as junk.

Naturally, the specific collector doesn't consider his stuff in derogatory terms, at least at first. You really can't positively identify what is junk until a few months after you buy it. If at that time, when you go look in your garage and your first thought when you see it is "what a piece of junk," then you know for sure what you have. It is at that point that most collectors become dealers and attempt to sell these "valuable treasures" to someone else.

We have the great good fortune to live in what may be the antiquing capital of the country. Part of the reason is that most of us in New Hampshire are too cheap to ever throw anything away, and, most importantly, we have basements and attics in which to store stuff. The basic dictum that the truly astute New Hampshire native lives by is:

"No matter how useless a piece of junk is, if you store it long enough, you can usually find some bozo to buy it."

And, as we all know, in this country (especially during tourist season) there is no shortage of bozos.

Perhaps you are wondering just what kinds of stuff the average antiqueophile collects. The answer is anything. There is of course the standard stuff like furniture, books, glassware, etc. But there are also nut cases out there who collect almost anything.

The following are some examples of obscure stuff which is listed regularly in the more popular antique price guides: table fans, Pez dispensers, barbed wire, old dental tools, toothpicks, mustache cups (left-handed ones are particularly valuable), pot lids, spittoons, chamber pots, doorknobs, flue covers, electrical insulators, potato mashers (those spelled with an "e" on the end are particularly rare), glove stretchers, fruit jars, eyecups, lunch boxes and light bulbs.

One could spend years trying to develop a pattern of behavior which links people with what they collect. Suffice it to say, you know people who collect some of these things, whether they will admit it or not. I admit to collecting one of these items myself (the only one that makes sense).

It is fun to speculate on what people do with some of this stuff.

How would you like to be married to a guy who collects old dental tools? Is he a dentist? Does he try his new "finds" out on his patients? Is that how he cuts costs? If you see an old chisel and pliers on the counter the next time you go for a check-up, you might want to consider checking out.

Or how about the person who collects old chamber pots. Where have these things been? If you're a guest at his or her house and ask to use the facilities, will you be handed one? Are they saving water? Will you know how to operate one? Are you expected to clean it?

Another of my favorites is barbed wire. Apparently there are a lot of different types. Can you imagine storing this stuff. Do you use it to keep the wife and kids out of your study when you're surfing the net? Or do you place it around the house in strategic locations to make it tough on burglars?

If you are feeling a little down about the economy and want a chance to feel richer, hop in the car and go out to Northwood or some other antique locale. For the casual observer, the group shops are the best. These shops have items for sale from a large number of different dealers, and you can find all sorts of items. I guarantee that you will find something in there that you own and always considered worthless junk but were too lazy to throw away. When you look at the price on it you will feel much richer. Of course, if it's an item that you finally badgered your spouse into taking to the dump last week, you may not feel so good.

For those of you who really get into the fun of antiquing, you will soon think about traveling to the big outdoor shows that occur all over New England in the summer. The largest, by far, is at Brimfield in Massachusetts. It is not far from Sturbridge Village and is held three times a year. Thousands of dealers come to this show and display their valuable stuff in huge open fields.

If you want to see a true cross-section of the antiquing population, this is the place to be. People are wearing strange hats and sandwich boards declaring what they collect. Cowbells and portable PA systems announce collectors of everything from poker chips to baseball memorabilia. Couples work in teams that spread out over miles with their cellphones on alert. Old ladies run people down in their three-wheel bikes attached to little wagons. You will see guys staggering down the street carrying tables, headboards, kitchen cabinets and easy chairs. And you will see refugees collapsed alongside the road while their spouses go on without them.

This is what makes America great. The coming together of greed, insanity, overindulgence, innovation, impatience, curiosity and passion, all rolled into one giant powerball of humanity. Ultimately, most of the participants will be thrown back out of the maelstrom holding something they consider a wonderful treasure. And many do this for several days in a row. It is true that most of them are certifiable but we shouldn't be too judgmental. After all, there are some perfectly sane people that also frequent some of these shows, looking for truly valuable stuff, like playing cards and lunch boxes. You know, things that actually indicate a collector with extraordinary taste.

Oh yes, and don't forget the garage sales, if you really start to like the idea of antiquing. But be careful. Some of these people are very grumpy in the morning and will thrash you silly if you get between them and an electrical insulator. ◆

Camping

MY DAUGHTERS, who have both reached voting age, have recently been giving me a lot if grief because I never took them camping when they were younger.

Whenever the subject of camping trips would come up around the dinner table in those early years, my wife would smile sweetly and tell us to "have a good trip." I knew what those words meant. They were a brazen attempt to have a little air-conditioned free time, while I picked up the cooking, cleaning and baby-sitting chores in bug-infested woods. My wilderness experience didn't let me down at those critical moments, however, and when the kids would excitedly ask when we were going, I would quickly change the subject, or work a compromise such as pitching a tent in the back yard. There they could fight off mosquitoes and learn to use a flashlight while I watched the ball game in the sanctity of my home, and mom still did the cooking.

Now, however, these young women have reached the age where they can make their own decisions and go on their own camping trips. And since I really am a decorated veteran of real camping, unlike my wimpy wife, I thought it might be time to make them understand the important elements of being a true camper. Too often this concept is compromised as corporations and unscrupulous sales people try to sell novices all sorts of fancy gear that totally destroys the chance to actually bond with nature. As a veteran camper from the days of wooden stakes and floorless tents, and someone who camped everywhere from White Lake to White Ledge, I felt that I could no longer shirk my duties to at least give them a firm understanding of what camping is and what it is not.

Camping is not done within the confines of a wheeled vehicle where the major life problems to be solved are locating an electrical outlet and downloading sewage. People existing in this environment have sold out to the establishment and should be referred to as "recvers." Many of them, at one time were probably real campers, but they obviously got stupid as they got older.

A camp is also not a rustic looking home on a lake somewhere. If it can't be set up and broken down in less than an hour, it's too fancy to qualify. Nor is camping someplace you go to swim and sail and get bossed around by a bunch of counselers.

Real campers sleep in tents and cook over real fires (or maybe Coleman stoves). They walk in real woods, use real latrines and bathe in . . . well they bathe when they can, which is almost never.

The casual observer of today does not understand real camping. For purists like myself, there can be no compromises. You must go through a right of passage and remain true to the code. For me, it was the Great Nickerson State Park Flood of 1950. My father took us to the park on Cape Cod on a Saturday, and left to go back to work on Sunday night (with the car). We were to see him the following Friday after four fun-filled days of camping adventures. It began raining about two hours after he left. By Monday morning we had learned a critical lesson in real camping. Never set up in a creek bed. My four-year-old sister and I clung to our cots like life rafts as we watched most of our worldly possessions sweep past the front flaps and on towards the Atlantic ocean. It was still raining when my father returned on Friday night. My mother, who had spent four days on a cot with a seven-year-old and a four-year-old and no dry clothes, was very quiet when he returned. Which was strange because she was talking a lot when he was gone about just waiting for him to get back. I learned a lot of new words on that trip. Surprisingly, we took a lot of camping trips after that, but Dad didn't seem to have to go back to work during any of them.

None of this should deter a real camper, however. After all, the object is to get back to nature, to taste the outdoors and live close to it like our ancestors. One of the problems for many people is taking too much equipment. A real camper uses cooking fires or kerosene stoves, and brings tarps and tents, sleeping bags, flashlights and canteens. He or she does not bring extraneous stuff like boom boxes, hair dryers, electrical appliances, or anything that attaches or hooks to a car.

One of the key rules in camping is to choose your fellow campers wisely. Some people are just not cut out to be real campers. If they are bringing iPads, frozen foods or beach umbrellas, trust your instincts. If they are bringing large quantities of alcoholic beverages, you have chosen wisely.

Once you have selected an area, pick your site carefully. My father paid dearly for his slight miscalculation in locating us in a creek bed. On subsequent trips, he always spent an extra hour digging a large trench around our tent. This was kind of a penance thing.

If you are truly in the wilds, your trenching tool will also serve to build a latrine. Make sure you build it downhill and downwind. Also it should be placed far enough away that you don't hear small indiscretions, yet close enough so you can hear loud panicky screams from those foolish enough to wander off in the night. If your camping area is one of those fancy ones with facilities, don't let small children go unattended. I nearly disappeared down one at age nine. If the facilities have flush toilets, you are disqualified as a real camper.

Once your tent is properly set up, you can enjoy the wonders of Mother Nature. Remember that a lot of the wildlife is small and fragile. But also keep in mind that some are voracious, plentiful and very tricky. For any true camper, the smell of the wild has a strong similarity to insect repellant. This is the most important item on the trip. If you forget the bug juice, be prepared to die a horrible death.

If you are fortunate enough to camp near a mountain stream, it will add a lot of ambience to your visit. It will keep your drinks cold and generally refresh you. Splash your face in it, dip your feet, but only bathe in it if your body odor is so bad that flowers are wilting as you pass. Men who bathe in mountain streams will talk in a high squeaky voice for days, and women will find that after a quick dip they will be able to travel at night without flashlights.

When dinnertime comes, be prepared for cold meals. Most of the time the parks people will get irritated with campfires. They are only really legal in times of flooding or total downpours. My personal recommendation after eating MRE's and a wide assortment of dried foods is to use your cellphone and order a pizza.(Yes, it is okay to bring one cellphone for these kinds of emergencies). If you insist on cooking, get out the Coleman stove, but be selective about what you cook. My Dad used to insist on hot dogs and baked beans every Saturday night. Even at age eight or nine I was smart enough to go sleep in the car on those nights.

When you are finished eating, always hang your food up off the ground. That way only the big animals can get it. If something is heard stealing your food during the night, send out the most expendable member of your party to investigate.

A message to my daughters. Never share your sleeping bag with anyone. For the rest of you, never share your sleeping bag with anyone with cold feet or small kidneys. If you must share your sleeping bag, always let the other person get in first. If they get back out very fast, carefully check the ID's of whatever wildlife is visiting.

Once you are in your bag, keep a flashlight close by in case you have to make a trip to the latrine. It is dark in the woods at night and the latrine monster is always lurking nearby. Make it a quick trip. If you are the first one up in the morning, be careful where you step when you come out of the tent. Sometimes the latrine monster is just too close and six year olds choose other options.

If it rains more than two days in a row, go home. It has been scientifically proven that no relationship can survive three days of rain, in a small tent. I believe my father is only alive today because he had the good sense to be back in Stoneham during the Great Flood.

I hope this will be a valuable reference source for my daughters as they strike out on their own camping expeditions. They should enjoy this stuff while they are young, because, soon enough, the rigors will become sufficiently daunting that they will have to take the high road, as I did, and blame their inaction on someone else, or they will be tempted to follow the low road . . . in a Winnebago. ◆

Searching for Customer Service

New Hampshire used to be a plain-speaking, down-to-earth place where we did business with a nod and a handshake. We sorted out our customer service problems directly. If we had a question, needed to change an address or wanted to discuss an issue, we picked up the phone and talked to a real live New Hampshire person. Life was simple.

The demise of customer service really occurred when some evil geniuses invented the "decision tree" automatic answering systems. These systems suddenly provided both corporate America and government bureaucracies with an unlimited number of degrees of separation from the customer. They found that extensive use of these devices almost completely eliminated any real communication with the customer. For many of these companies, the systems have allowed them to replace their customer service departments with a well-trained cockatoo, and reassign critical human resources to such pressing issues as developing new bonus plans and redesigning forms.

Installing these systems has resulted in dramatically reducing customer complaints. This has been accomplished by initiating a diabolically clever war of attrition with the consumer. The first assault is to task the caller with fifty or sixty button-pushing decisions. Hardly anyone over sixty is going to even remember why they called after being put through eight decision trees. This immediately eliminates many of the callers who don't have enough spare time to actually proceed through this jungle.

Unfortunately, I was faced with an issue that could only be resolved directly, and I was forced to continue through this maze. The next step in the process was to be told that I would be allowed to speak to a real person in "x" number of minutes. I learned after the first couple of tries to multiply this number by six. A word of caution to novices: if the first waiting time they give you is more that ten minutes, that is their secret code for "we have gone home for the night." Do not try to outwait them in this circumstance because the phone is automatically programmed to disconnect you after eight minutes. Their final ploy while you are waiting is to assault you with a carefully selected assortment of brain-numbing music, designed to turn you into a vegetable. This will leave you on an IQ level with whomever you finally speak to.

I survived this test by just leaving the phone off the hook on my desk until I heard a voice. When I finally reached a live person, I explained that I was calling to have the phone company disconnect a phone that was in the name of my recently deceased father. I was told in broken English that they would only speak to my father regarding this issue, and then they hung up. Accepting this challenge in the true New Hampshire spirit, I redialed, went through the whole process again and then told them I was my father and I needed to cancel my phone because I was dead.

They were fine with that. Given the waiting periods involved with these systems, it probably happens to them all the time. ◆

Thanks For the Clock and Everything Else

In keeping with the needs of a new year, apparently we now have a new topic to complain about. The keepers of the flame of controversy, are once again serving notice on the city that Good Samaritans, Scouts of both genders, gentle strangers and caring citizens should enter our community at their own risk.

There should be a Concord equivalent of the "Miranda" warning given at our borders that says something like the following. "If you knowingly try to do anything that actually benefits this community, you shall be subject to attack by angry crowds. You shall have the right to psychiatric help, and you will need it. You may be tarred and feathered, and your intentions subverted, but only after being ridiculed, castigated, and run over by a truckload of torch-carrying protestors complaining about almost everything, and chanting repeatedly that no good deed will go unpunished."

The subject of the latest anger is the clock that has been erected just off of Eagle Square. This large old clock hung above the downtown for many years in another era. Some good fortune and hard work salvaged it just as it was about to disappear forever. Pieces of the clock and the bell were scattered around the country in the late eighties, when the first "Save the Clock" group managed to raise enough money to get the pieces back together and donate them to the community. It then sat in storage for several years before another group raised the money to restore it to its current beautiful condition and place it in the downtown.

Now that we have this piece of history back, it's time to break out the verbal ax handles and beat up everyone involved. People complain that they have watches, or other clocks in town, why do we need this one. Or, presumably after eating Christmas dinner, they grump that the sidewalk is too narrow at the location where they put it. (For the record, the space, at its most narrow opening, is just as wide as some other sections of the concrete sidewalk that covers most of downtown.) Or the clockworks are enclosed so you can't stand in there to get out of the rain. Or it blocks the view of one part of a branch of the black metal tree sculpture that straddles the opening to Eagle Square. (There are also people who regularly sit or stand in front of that tree. I guess we need to remove them as well.) I am sure that more complaints will follow. Someone will try to use it as an ATM and claim they couldn't get their money. A homeless person will take up residence in it, and demand running water and electricity. A Generation Xer will request that it be converted to digital. A PC policeman will want us to get rid of the Roman numerals on the grounds that it demeans all Italians by implying they don't know how to use real numbers. The architectural denizens will complain that the shelter's old-fashioned design doesn't reflect our place in the modern world.

I would assume that we might also see a group of citizens show up at the next city council meeting demanding to know why the location wasn't on a referendum. After all, how can we entrust such an important decision to our elected representatives? And let's have three or four open meetings, so we can build up a groundswell of opposition from everyone who has had a bad day this century. And above all, let's make sure we trash everyone involved with putting this stupid clock there in the first place.

Okay. Enough with the sarcasm. Let's get serious for a minute. This community has had a lot of people who have donated time and energy to a variety of projects that have helped to make this city the vibrant, enjoyable place that it is. The efforts to save this clock spanned two decades and involved hard work from a great many people. This is the same type of effort that saved the Capital Centre for the Arts, built Dillon Field and Red River Theatre, put the weathervane on the old Firehouse block, got us the fountains in Eagle Square and Bicentennial Square, created Rotary Park out at Sewall's Falls Dam, and built the Hospice House. These things don't happen by accident and most of us feel they have provided positive benefits to the community. So perhaps we could take a time out from trashing everything in sight just because we can. Maybe we could even step back and thank all of these members of the community for trying to make this a better place.

None of us agree with everything that our community does. Certainly I am as guilty as anyone is about finding things that the city needs to do better. I try, however, to make it constructive or at least a little humorous. And I try never to lose track of how hard most of the people in this community, including the elected representatives, and city employees, work to make this such a fine place to live.

I guess what really saddened me about this latest controversy, is just how discouraging it can be for people to work so long and hard to accomplish something and then not even be able to enjoy a few moments of satisfaction. All of us need that, especially volunteers. Let's give each other a little credit once in a while. To all of you who worked from those early difficult days to final completion, on all of these projects and the many I have failed to mention, please go to the mirror right now and look with pride at someone who has helped to make this a better place. And please don't get discouraged about tackling new projects just because we may give you a little grief.

And the next time someone tells you they screwed up the clock shelter because there aren't any restrooms in it, or you can't drive your pickup down the sidewalk next to it, just smile and remember that you at least now have finally found a good reason for learning your Roman numerals in grade school. ◆

Smelly Dog Story

My recent experiences have led me to believe that the range of specialist care in our community leaves much to be desired. In particular I am referring to the areas of dermatology and cardiac, ophthalmological and psychiatric expertise. The result has been to create a situation where the patients have to travel miles for special care and where the loved ones are subjected to cruel and unusual punishment. I am, of course, referring to the level of specialist care for the dogs of our fair city.

Let me give you just one example of how onerous this situation can be for dog owners and their little friends.

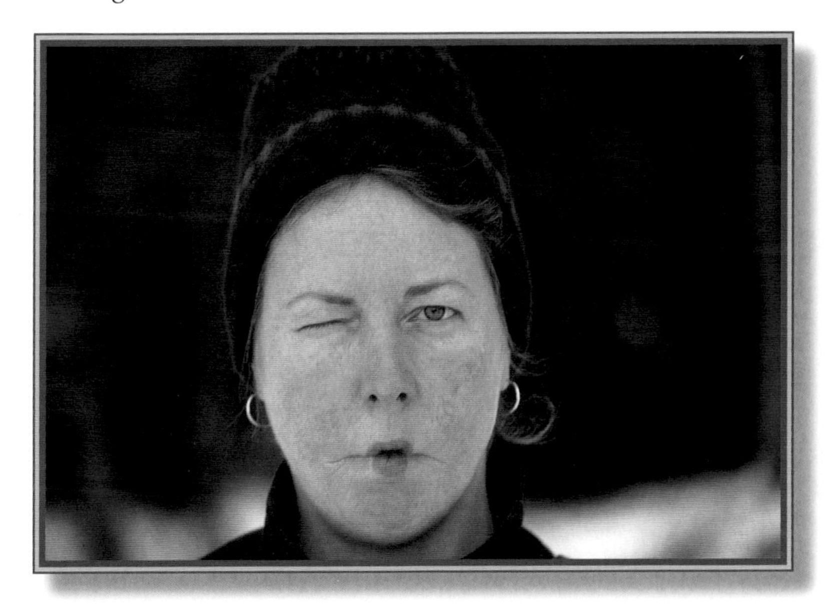

A few years ago we acquired custody of an old dog. He came to us via my mother-in-law, who greatly loves him, but is not currently in a position to care for him. This dog, a miniature poodle named Cromwell, is of gentle, friendly and lovable disposition, but I fear, limited intelligence. (Perhaps an unfair observation based on his willingness to eat rocks and pistachio nut shells.)

He is, as I have said, an old dog, currently in his sixteenth year, and he shares many of the problems familiar to humans of a comparable age. One particularly troubling issue that he had, however, was that he really stunk. I am not talking about your ordinary wet dog, skunk encounter or rolling in doodoo smell. We were looking at melt-the-furniture, burn-the-clothing type odor.

We tried everything. We used doggie-sized odor eaters, sprayed him with Febreze and hung little bottles of Renuzit around his neck. We bathed him in shampoo that smelled like tropical fruit, until it got on him and then gave off the odor of five-day-old flounder. We knew it was getting bad when two Jehovah's Witnesses nearly passed out just standing at our front door. (Interestingly, we haven't had any more visits from this group.)

Finally one of the general practitioners in town, while wearing a mask, suggested we take him to a doggie dermatologist in Hanover. This was my first realization that such specialists existed, but you can imagine my disappointment to find that she was an hour away.

In desperation we decided to make the trip. We loaded Crom into the car and began the loooong journey. In the first five minutes we realized we needed gas, and Susanne and I raced to see who would get out first to refuel the car and thus enjoy the relatively wholesome odor of gas fumes for a few minutes. I won, but she is still bitter.

Once we were on our way, it became apparent that although the temperature was twenty-two degrees, we would be making the trip with the windows and the sunroof open. Several passing cars slowed and stared at the sight of two humans hanging their heads out the windows while the dog sat at quiet attention in the back seat. (Cromwell would have joined us, I am sure, except that his back legs are no longer strong enough to support him getting up to the window.)

In Hanover, the doggie dermatologist gave him antibiotics, a special vegetable diet (yum!), and different shampoos. She also suggested we see a doggie ophthalmologist in Boston and a doggie psychiatrist somewhere in Connecticut (I think). I suggested we leave the dog with her for observation, but she just gave me one of those little smiles that said, "don't even go there."

We (barely) survived the trip back and the dog's odor has gradually returned to the more normal level of "meadow muffin ripe."

My point in relating all of this is that because we don't have these specialists available in Concord, Susanne and I were forced to make a very perilous trip to Hanover, during which we could have passed out at any moment, endangering ourselves, our pet and other drivers.

I am sure other pet owners have faced similar daunting experiences. We need to have these services available locally. I can tell you from personal experience that there is a pressing need for doggie psychiatrists, and an hour is too far to drive when green fumes start emanating from your pet.

I call on dog owners of the city to unite and demand these services for our community. ◆

The Farmers' Market

IN THE LAST FEW YEARS, I have been a regular participant in the farmers' market in Concord. It has been a lot of fun and has allowed me to be in a position to share with you some observations on the preferences and habits of many of our citizens as seen through the prism of one of our state's ancient and honored traditions.

These markets provide New Hampshire's soul food. And satisfied souls they are. A couple of weeks ago I saw thirty-five pies disappear out of one booth in about two and a half hours. Fresh bread, pastries, muffins, and brownies are everywhere. Almost every child at the market has chocolate, some kind of jam or cookie crumbs on their face. (An unofficial poll that I did last week would suggest that chocolate is still the flavor of choice among New Hampshire kids, with cookie crumb a close second.)

If you are a first timer at the market, please do not stand idly near any veggie booths once the butter and sugar corn comes out. You will be trampled. Those unfortunate enough to arrive after the last basket of corn has been emptied are a disgruntled lot indeed. Usually they seek solace at the pastry booths. Take the kids and clear the area if they are also sold out.

Clothing options at the market are many and varied, and provide a pretty accurate view of the priorities of New Hampshire's citizens. You will see everything from suspenders and plaid shirts to an occasional silk sari, and from work boots to plastic clogs. What you will not see, is anything out of the pages of *Vogue*. While New Hampshire may be number one in the nation in common sense, our fashion sense probably ranks somewhere below North Dakota.

Extended observation of this cross-section of our citizens also makes it clear why New Hampshire should always be the site of the first in the nation primary. People actually stop and say hello to each other and talk about real life. That same approach has been proven over the years to carry into their conversation with the candidates. Our future presidents are going to get more than an *Entertainment Tonight* questioning. As you watch our citizens walking around the market, you realize that they can quickly recognize a bad ear of corn or a soft melon. And that knowledge can cut down dramatically on the bad produce people try to ship to Washington. Of course, if all the country brings to our market is zucchini . . .

Overall, the farmers' markets give you a pretty good feeling that New Hampshire is still in touch with its history and that many of our priorities are still pretty well grounded in the common sense for which we take great pride. Certainly there is something to be said for people who can recognize a good piece of pastry, and still revel in wonderful homemade pies. And let's face it, when it comes to New Hampshire corn in season, nothing should get in the way of a citizen and the back of the farmer's truck. ◆

Thanks for the Worries

RECENTLY MY RADIO blared out at me with an advertisement for the treatment of a newly defined disease. It was described as "generalized anxiety syndrome."

Upon further analysis it became clear that we were really talking about a fancy name for people who worry too much. I don't classify this as a new illness since I've been suffering from it for years. Of course I didn't know I had a disease. I thought I just worried too much. Now I can worry about a disease.

Even better, the advertiser says he has a new experimental drug to treat the disease. So I can also worry about whether I should take the drug. I can also worry about why, if this drug is so good, they are desperately advertising for volunteers. After all, almost everyone I know worries too much. And who can blame them.

Our national capability to worry is almost unlimited. And it is strongly reinforced by media that is not happy unless they are pushing the public panic button.

The material to do this is plentiful and I have put together just a small sampling of the basic equal-opportunity worries that assault our senses. I have purposely left off this list the really well-known concerns such as smoking, AIDS, high blood pressure, cancer, etc., which are actual real worries. Instead, I am going to focus on the vaguer, hit and run issues that the media seem to assault us with on an almost daily basis.

First on the list is food. I don't have a clue what I should be eating. It used to be that if it tasted good and was fattening, it was bad for you. If it had the flavor of cardboard, you could eat as much as you wanted.

There was lots of guidance from trusted authority figures. Do you remember when your mother told you to drink your milk? You just knew it was good for you. She never said, "Drink your Coke." Life was simple.

Then came the media blitz, however, in which the nation's favorite baby doctor and some cronies declared that milk was a national disaster. Every TV news show and newspaper in the country picked up the story and ran with it.

Of course, some might have been a little skeptical since Dr. Spock was also the guy responsible for the upbringing of all the bubble-headed idiots who became known as the Sixties Generation (of which I must confess to be one).

Dr. Spock, and a triumvirate of milk "experts," hit us with a massive scare that left the milk industry in tatters, and then nothing. Nobody gave us alternatives (except breast milk, which is a little tough to come by for a fifty-year-old). And nobody had the courage to step up and tell us that these guys were a couple of pints short of a quart. Instead the subject just suddenly disappeared from the news. It was a hit and run attack on milk that left us worrying without resolution.

Milk is not alone among foods to worry about, however. Sometime over the last couple of decades, the following foods have been declared dangerous to consume: tomatoes, cranberries, grapes, apples, sugar, salt, chicken, beef, all dairy products, swordfish, all processed foods, anything wrapped in plastic, margarine, peanut butter, chocolate, white flour, happy meals and coffee, to name just a few.

That covers almost everything I like, and I know I've missed a lot. There's also some stuff I'm not sure about. Oat bran used to be good, then it was bad or neutral. I don't know. I don't care.

But let's not focus on food worries. There's a whole smorgasboard of stuff to get us into a panic.

1) Air and water (loaded with pollutants)
2) Sunshine (UV exposure)
3) Televisions, microwaves, electric blankets (radiation)

4) Cell phones (brain cancer)
5) Male pattern baldness (heart attacks)
6) Breast implants (silicone)
7) Charlie Sheen raising children

The list is endless.

So what's the solution? I'm not sure, but I suspect it doesn't start with taking some experimental drug, unless you want to know what you'll be worrying about next.

Basically, it seems we all need to lighten up a little. Maybe the media need to stop the hit and run attacks. Perhaps they should even consider the source, before they start publishing allegations. After all, in this country you can get some loony tune to make any kind of absurd statement, and if it is repeated enough in the right places, it will achieve some level of credibility.

There are also some things we might be better off not knowing. What am I going to do about it, even if it is true that losing my hair makes me a higher risk candidate for a heart attack. The ensuing anxiety probably jumps my odds another 100 percent.

The public also needs to use a little common sense. (I know this is a toughie.)I mean guys were calling their doctors after the news came out to see if they could eliminate the heart attack threat by having a hair transplant. Maybe a head transplant would work.

As for the food issues, maybe we should go back to eating what we like. We're going to worry about it anyway, so at least let's have a good time. If it turns out we did eat the wrong thing, we can always clean the system out real good by turning on C-Span and watching Washington politics at work. Now that is something to worry about. ◆

The Challenge of Meetings

As I continue to distance myself from age fifty, I am finding a steady stream of additional burdens that those of us who have passed that magic mark seem to share. One of these is that I am having an increasingly difficult time staying awake in meetings, presentations and speeches.

And, as I look around me, while attending these events, and before my thought processes begin to blur, I can see others, generally also over fifty, wrestling with the same difficulty. I see a gentleman facing the wrong way at his table during a luncheon speech, clearly doing some serious introspection. And I see another, hovering dangerously over a plate of mashed potatoes.

I understand that certain speakers and subjects can bring out these tendencies even in younger participants, but it seems to strike more frequently now that I have passed my golden birthday. I have been trying to determine why this inclination towards "meeting somnolence" seems to afflict those of us over fifty more extensively. (Maybe it is partly the result of too many speakers using words like a couple of those in the last sentence.)

After some careful analysis, I believe I have isolated a few factors that may contribute to why we are more susceptible than younger people to this malady.

Those of us over fifty have already had to sit through a lot of these darn things.

I think most of us are more tired. (Hey, I didn't say this was rocket science.)

In an informal survey, 98 percent of us hate acronyms and speeches laced with PC (politically correct) double talk or bureaucratic word-speak that advocates intelligence-challenged protocols, requiring interventions and consensus-building. (No matter how many cups of coffee I have had, I am going to lose my focus and go comatose after about thirty seconds of this stuff.)

Because there is some justification, as listed above, for our condition, the good news is that when you get past fifty, people have a tendency to excuse a few sleep indiscretions.

This basically means that fellow attendees will generally ignore, perhaps even envy, you as long as your head doesn't hit the table hard enough to break china, and you don't snore too loud.

In business, I have seen some absolute masters at "meeting sleep." My first boss in civilian life had perfected this skill to its zenith. He sat through almost all meetings with his eyes closed, so no one knew whether he concentrated better with his eyes shut, or just slept a lot. I learned that he had a remarkable ability to keep a mental tape recorder going so that, almost invariably, when asked a question at a meeting, he could answer it. After several years of observation, I realized that I could tell if he was really sleeping by how long it took him to answer. If he had to stare off into space for a while, demonstrating deep thought, and maybe did the " church and steeple" thing with his hands, I knew that he was having to rerun that tape recorder back a fair distance to get a true sense of the discussion leading up to the question. It was a skill that required a special and perhaps unique genius, and the man was one of my idols as I learned the ways of the business world. A young man, however, could never have pulled this off. Young guys have to keep their eyes open at business meetings.

Another amazing display of successfully converting meeting time to sleep time was demonstrated by one of my own employees in Houston a few years ago. He was a fifty-five year old hardened field operator whom I had brought back from one of our Saudi Arabian projects. He was a veteran of some of the most boring meetings on the planet. Those were held in Saudi Arabia and involved twenty to twenty-five people. They were conducted almost entirely in Arabic, generally lasted three to four hours, and required almost no contribution from English-speaking westerners. When he came back to Houston, he was required to sit in on our operational meetings. He had a reputation for being taciturn and lived up to it. But halfway through the second meeting I asked him a question and got nothing. He was sitting there staring at the table, but it was like he was dead. A hand waved in front of his face didn't even draw a blink. We were about to dial 911 when the commotion woke him up. He had absolutely perfected the art of sleeping sitting up with his eyes open. Since he was older and valuable in many other ways, he could get away with it. In fact, he also got out of most of our meetings since his presence could be distracting and a little creepy.

While I find myself now facing the same problem, I don't possess any of the special skills of these gentlemen. I only have the standard defenses and they aren't working as well anymore. I used to be able to drink five or six cups of coffee and be confident it would enable me to endure any meeting. Now, however, after six cups of coffee, I spend half the day in the bathroom. I've also found that this can have a negative snowball effect, because certain unscrupulous people will take the opportunity when you are out of a meeting, to appoint you to additional committees where you will have to attend even more meetings.

I also used to go stand in the back of the room if my eyes were really starting to glaze. Because of the severity of recent nap attacks, however, I now worry that I'll lose my balance back there and incur serious injury.

In a desperate effort of self-preservation, I would therefore like to make the following suggestions/pleas to speakers, presenters, and callers of meetings:

Don't darken the room after people have eaten.

Try to avoid using nouns as verbs, or speaking in the language of acronyms and abbreviations. This can lead to MEGOizing your audience. (If you don't know what MEGO means, you haven't attended enough meetings.)

Only speak to groups in rooms where the temperature is below 40 degrees. That way if we fall asleep we risk freezing to death. (Fear is a good stimulant.)

If you must drone on interminably, do it quietly, and don't make any sudden moves or loud sounds. (People can get injured and a lot of the potential victims in this town are lawyers.)

If you are doing a dinner speech, never start it after 8:00 p.m. If I were home, I would probably already be asleep on the couch. An uncomfortable chair and indigestion at 9:00 p.m. will just make me a grumpy sleeper.

Oh yeah, and finally, if you call a meeting, please make your point, get the decision and get out of there. And if someone looks like they are doing some deep thinking, leave them alone and let them sleep. ◆

Multitasking

MULTITASKING MAY HAVE SAVED civilization as we now know it. Given all the wonderful new electronic toys that have been developed over the last thirty years, it doesn't seem like it would be possible to fit their full usage into a twenty-four hour day without our citizens' remarkable ability to become skilled at multitasking.

Think of how difficult it would be to devote proper attention to all our computers, cellphones, televisions, video games and iPods, if our inventiveness hadn't made many of these electronic wonders capable of performing many tasks at the press of a button.

Our modern society has essentially ended the need for stereos, VCRs, CD players, DVDs, pagers, paper notebooks, calculators, typewriters, fax machines, copiers, compasses, telephones (landlines), encyclopedias, books, newspapers and games requiring other people in the same room. All of these can now be easily replaced by a portable computer, an up-to-date cellphone, and/or an iPad. And each of them is gradually doing more of the work of the others. You can talk for hours, practically free, on computers, watch shows on cellphones and iPads, and do your word processing by just talking to one of your electronic toys.

People have learned to use these simultaneously. Now they can check email, stay current on the latest soaps and reality TV, commute on the turnpike, dictate reports to the office while receiving a fax from overseas, scream at the guy cutting them off at the exit and write (text) to a friend. In previous eras, it would have taken hours to get all that done.

Things actually began to change with the proliferation of fast food places and the invention of the microwave. Once the need to cook dinner on a real stove was eliminated, it opened up all sorts of additional time for families. Everyone could get home later, eat faster, and waste less time actually communicating with each other. Then we got remote controls on the TVs so guys could watch three different sporting events at once. This in turn forced wives and kids to get their own TVs, which further cut down on face time.

The arrivals of all the new electronic toys were initially a challenge, but with the reduced need to communicate with real people, we began to see evolution take hold. Our fingers became more dexterous as we learned to use them for video games, channel flipping and text messaging.

Our Blackberries became cellphones, cameras and pagers, our automobiles became portable offices and movie theaters, our computers became capable of video conference calls and "Skyping," and they all talked to each other. Pretty soon we didn't even need to get involved in some of the conversations.

For many, there is almost no reason for real life to intrude on these virtual worlds. Messy issues such as meeting people face-to-face, having real conversations with our children and meeting our neighbors need never occur. Even the survival of the species can be assured without the need for face-to-face meetings.

But if you are still of the old school that favors some contact in this last critical objective, our inventive geniuses have developed easy ways to multitask this as well. This was clearly pointed out in a television commercial a while ago. Modern man was busy playing with his remote control and waiting for a big game when his wife signaled that it might be time for a little face-to-face contact. What to do! Then he remembered the opportunities provided by multitasking. He could TIVO the big game, take a Viagra and spend some quality time with his wife without missing anything important, or getting too emotionally involved. In a final tribute to multitasking, it is possible he also combined it with dining on a well-rounded meal of edible underwear.

Some of you out there may think this is the beginning of the end of our civilization. But most of us in New Hampshire don't get too caught up in this stuff. We may use many of these new marvels, but we still find plenty of time to spend with our families, watch a sunset, count the stars and get to know our neighbors, right?

And if not, it's not really that big a deal. I know some web sites that have great pictures of the galaxies and sunsets, and there are several that will send greetings to friends and relatives free of charge. As for the neighbors, most of them are too busy to want to meet you anyway. And that gives you more time to pour a cool drink, go out to the screened-in porch and update your Facebook. ◆

A Call to Arms

THE FOLLOWING IS ADDRESSED to the men of New Hampshire, who, for the most part, need a call to arms . . . and legs and abs and everywhere else.

While I know that many of you believe that preparing for winter involves piling on layers of fat and hibernating until spring, there is some scientific evidence that indicates this may not be the best approach to good health. Sure, it could work pretty well until football season is over, but then what? Three months of watching pro basketball, figure skating and reality TV?

Wouldn't it be nice to spend that three months actually working on making a six pack instead of seeing how many you can drink? All right, maybe I am overstepping the bounds of reality a little, but come on, admit it, at sometime in your life you have wondered how it would feel to have a really ripped body. Wouldn't you like to get off the couch without help and be able to grunt and groan in three syllables?

Well today is the day. After a few years of "pumping iron," and learning everything the hard way, I have decided to give you the benefit of my experience and provide you with a beginner's guide to weight lifting.

Read this carefully and you could soon be on the road to the fitness adventure of a lifetime. (Be advised, however, that the path usually runs through a really smelly gym with bad ventilation.)

The first thing you need is to be able to speak the special language that is unique to us iron aficionados. I am assuming that most of you are of above-average intellect (since you can read) so this should not be a difficult task. Mostly, it consists of shorthand references to various parts of the body like "pecs" and "quads" (pectorals and quadriceps), but sometimes it gets a little more complicated by adding "-ie" to it such as pulling "hammies" (hamstrings). You should not get carried away with the "-ie" thing. They don't talk about "peccies" and "gluties" and "latties," nor would it be good to apply it to clothing items like pants and shorts. Your knowledge of anatomy doesn't have to be too extensive because most lifters have a universal code for complicated stuff. When they injure unknown places, they just swear a lot and start holding the damaged body part.

You also need to know the special names for the weights. For instance the circular metal round things that you put on the end of the bars are known by their poundage. Nickels, dimes and quarters are pretty self-explanatory. (Hint: If you can't figure this out, you are too stupid to pursue weight lifting, which would make you very special and probably qualify you for the *Guinness Book of Records*.) The tricky weight is the "plate," which is forty-five pounds. Since we don't have a forty-five-cent coin, one can only speculate as to the origin of this name. I am guessing it is probably the size of the dish that holds the meals that some of these guys put away after a workout. For some reason, forty-five pounds has special significance among lifters. The normal big bar also weighs that same amount. Perhaps it has something to do with metric systems, since it is about twenty kilograms or a little over three stone. However, since no one there had a clue exactly how much a gram or a stone really is, that theory was quickly dismissed. This is apparently a need-to-know thing and no one in my gym needed to know. So it remains simply a plate.

The rest of the special gym language consists mostly of multisyllabic grunts, groans and squeals that take years to understand. The only one of these that you probably need to learn quickly is the high-pitched gurgle/squeal that is emitted when a guy has lifted too much and now has a heavy bar resting on his throat.

Now that you know the language, you are ready to do some actual lifting. My first piece of advice here is to wear lots of clothes. There are mirrors everywhere, and as a beginner, you don't want to see what you really look like. The veteran lifters love these mirrors. They stand in front of them dressed in "muscle shirts," with heavy weights hanging off the bars, admiring their clean and jerks. An unspoken rule is "don't get between a lifter and his mirror."

As a new lifter you should find a quiet corner and work on some light weights. Perhaps you could start with a pair of nickel hand weights. Do not mess with the colored or rubberized weights. Find the ugliest, most evil-looking, rusted, blackish iron weights you can locate. Remember that you are now a macho guy who is out to pump some iron, not squeeze some plastic. If all they have are plastic-coated weights, it means you are in one of those sissy gyms where some of the members wear color-coordinated outfits, and where women are seen in great numbers. A word of caution here. Many of the women in these places will tell you they are just out to tone their bodies. Don't believe them. If they have been there a while, they can probably lift you into the ground, and if you try to compete with them you will quickly be swearing and pointing to a broken body part. My recommendation is to tell them you are lifting "light" while recuperating from an injured quad/pec that happened when you were competing in last weeks car-throwing contest.

If you survive the first couple of weeks, you can gradually add some weight, and someone will probably clue you in on which exercises are good for which muscles. Remember, however, that none of these people can be trusted. Do not believe anything they say unless it is confirmed by at least two independent sources. Veteran lifters are a sadistic group who will enjoy watching you make a fool of yourself. Not that any of them were able to do that to me. Nor do I harbor any lingering resentment about the scale incident.

Never forget that, except for you, most lifters are crazy. Who else would spend useful waking hours moving dead weights around a room, while making their eyes bug out. (One of the high points of any lifting session is watching the faces some of these guys make when they are pushing their limits.) Once you have accepted the fact that these guys are nuts, however, it gets easier. They can be a scary-looking group, but most of the ones in my group spend a lot more time trash-talking than actually lifting. And they are not as macho as you might think. An example would be the other day when I was down at the other end of the gym doing some real lifting, and I noticed four of them standing around, as usual, engaged in a heated discussion. I wandered down to commend them on achieving a talk to lift ratio of 20:1, when I noticed that the argument was over the virtues of a front-loading washing machine versus a top-loader. This is not an acceptable weight lifter topic. This is a subject for discussion at a wedding shower or a women's knit night. I gently pointed this out to them in my most politically correct tone. When they realized the damage they had done to their images, they all scattered back to their weights like chastened schoolboys.

Finally, I also would like to advise you to stay away from group lifts. When these guys start to do "special" exercises, move to the other end of the gym. I still haven't figured out the purpose of all of these, but it reminds me of a fraternity hazing. The other day four of them were standing around one guy who is stretched between two benches on his back with his hands on the edge of one and his feet on the other in a position to do dips. Then these other guys drop two plates on his groin. After writhing in initial agony, he starts actually doing dips. While the group counts out loud, the guy's facial contortions indicate that they are ripping his heart out and feeding it to angry squirrels. Ultimately, he is reduced to a cringing mass of quivering flesh. Everyone then cheers. For veteran lifters, this kind of activity is as good as it gets.

One final word of caution. If you are thinking about hiring a personal trainer, remember that they are all unstable sadists who enjoy inflicting pain. You will be paying them to turn you into a psychotic masochist. My personal guess is that most of them are part of the Federal Witness Protection Program and used to work for the Russian Mafia.

I hope that this brief introduction has inspired you to head down to your local gym and sign up to be one of us. It's a great escape from the real world, lets you focus on the truly trivial and insignificant, and gives you the opportunity to still attain that childhood dream of "pumping iron." A winter of this stuff and you will know every muscle in your body, and maybe be able to get off the couch on your own. And who knows, maybe one day you could even become the governor of California! ◆

Basement Explorations

Because of the recent flooding, I was forced to confront the stuff in my basement. This is a scary process and something I generally avoid. But with water rising all around me, I was making frequent inspections and couldn't avoid focusing on what was down there. It wasn't pretty.

Susanne and I have different family histories. I come from a long line of careful savers, whereas Susanne's instincts are to throw stuff away before it is even opened. This was a definite culture clash when we first got married. I finally cured her of the unopened thing when I suggested that even obvious advertisements sometimes have good stuff in them. She said, "like what"? She then proceeded to open a piece of junk mail that had come in that day. Inside, as part of some survey, was a nice new dollar bill. What are the odds? But she always looks before she throws stuff away now.

She still loves to toss things out, however. Sometimes she does it just to watch me writhe in pain. I used to have a collection of old *Playboy* magazines from the 1950s to the 1970s that I was keeping as a reference library. (Many of our great American writers first published short stories in this esteemed journal.) One day the entire library disappeared. She confessed to the evil act after the trash collectors had come. She may have felt some remorse later when I showed her copies of those magazines selling for $25–30 in antique shops, but I fear she never truly regretted this rash affront to a treasured segment of Americana.

Since that regrettable incident, she has been more hesitant to act precipitously on her thrower instincts. The result has been that the savers in our family (me) have been relatively unimpeded in our accumulation of things as long as they wind up in the basement. As I surveyed the basement last month, however, even I had to admit that things might be getting out of hand.

I noted the presence of six old computers, two printers, three monitors, a black and white TV, a reel-to-reel tape deck, two old amplifiers, four speakers, plus the original boxes for most of this stuff. These are being saved primarily because I don't know what to do with them. They may be hazardous or toxic, have identity theft issues, or someone might need an old IBM XT someday.

We did try to donate some of them, but no organization was desperate enough to want old, worthless electronic equipment. Times must be pretty good at all the nonprofits in town. I am now contemplating giving them as gifts. I recently made a test run by unloading an old fertilizer spreader on a friend as a birthday present. I have no doubt this spreader will be regifted several times until, like the proverbial fruit cake, some worn out soul, preferably not me, will wind up losing it in the maze of their basement, where it will finally be unearthed in an archaeological dig a millennium from now.

Awakening from this philosophical musing, I took further inventory. I found six boxes of reference books, and forty cartons of old documents like tax data, brokerage statements, and boardroom reports, all of which date from the present back to the 1970s. I never know when to throw this stuff away because whenever I do, two weeks later someone will ask for it.

Other items found in my rummagings were an extensive collection of worthless Christmas presents, obviously given by desperate souls who I suspect were doing some regifting of their own. There are bags of things like old Chia pets, not quite broken Slinkys, various multipurpose kitchen appliances, and a surprisingly large number of plastic windup toys with feet.

There were also the standard things like old records, tapes, games, cookie tins, lamps, two old beds, and about 4,000 electronic connectors, chargers and power cords that go to nothing we actually use, but are in nearly mint condition.

Oh yeah, and since the *Playboy* debacle, we now have lots of magazines. These are carefully saved and will never be worth anything. None of the stuff accumulating now has anywhere near the same reference value. We closed the barn door on that particular collectible after all the bunnies had escaped.

As I surveyed the basement, I tried to prioritize what I would save first, if water started to pour in. This caused my head to ache, so I shut off the light and went to bed.

It turned out that all that worrying was for naught. The basement stayed dry and all that valuable stuff is still there. Does anyone need some electronic connectors, a six way vegetable chopper or some old Chia pets? ◆

Road Rage

THE LIGHT TURNED YELLOW and I slowed down. The light turned red and I stopped. The guy behind me turned purple. I thought maybe he was having a heart attack, but then I realized he was just angry at his steering wheel, which he kept hitting. The steering wheel cried for help, emitting some painful beeping sounds. Nobody went to its aid.

I guess I can understand his frustration. What was I thinking not to speed up and run that red light? I could have already been on the turnpike access road, unyielding in my movements and forcing the guy doing the speed limit in the right lane to jam on his brakes to make room for me. Too bad about the numbskull tailgating that guy. Besides, he could always have moved over a lane, except for that pea brain who was hanging off the guys left rear fender, cruising in his blind spot while texting on the phone with her boyfriend.

I don't know whether it's the economy, the long winters, too much coffee or the spreading urbanization of our state, but it strikes me that too many of us are becoming "city drivers." The problem with that is that we don't have city traffic to slow us down. We are doing a lot of the stupid city stuff at much higher speeds.

Having grown up in Massachusetts and lived in Houston for eight years, I know about dumb city driving. And having successfully survived all of that, I believe I can speak authoritatively on the subject. Therefore, as a public service to the few normal, sane individuals in this world (all of whom are reading this article), I thought it would be useful to provide some sensible driving hints to allow you to survive the daily encounters with the imbeciles that I describe as "city drivers."

Never believe a yield sign. No one ever yields at these things. Okay, once in 1986 I saw someone yield. She was hit from behind, dragged from her car and stoned to death in the middle of the rotary. Your only protection when encountering a yield sign and you have the right-of-way, is to get right out of the way. Clear a path for these interlopers and hope three of them don't come at you at once.

Merge signs are a sure indicator that things are about to get hostile. If you are in the primary lane, city drivers will always accelerate past you, go right up to the barrier and then, usually at full speed, cut you off. If you are in the lane that is ending and city drivers are already in the surviving lane, you will die there. You're only hope of ever getting into the primary lane is to wait for a tourist.

If someone cuts you off, forces you to jam on the brakes and spill half your coffee down your pants, and then makes an obscene gesture, don't start chasing him through traffic. What if you catch him? I mean the person is obviously deranged, he's driving a 4000-pound vehicle, and he is leading you at high speeds through traffic where half of those people are also nut jobs. And you will be one of them.

When starting up at a traffic light, count to ten after the light turns green before moving. In Houston we called this the "green count." We have so many people running red lights in Concord now, that you need that extra time to avoid the 18-wheelers, cement trucks and pickups that will be blowing through the intersection at 40 mph after the light has gone red. Remember the "red light corollary." The speed of traffic increases in inverse proportion to the time left before a light turns red. They will always be moving fastest at that point. The "green count" is also useful in helping you avoid wiping out the pedestrians on their cell phones who always step out into traffic just as your three-minute red light goes green for the allotted twenty seconds.

Never assume someone in a turn lane is going to turn. The insurance files are filled with claims from accidents caused by people doing the wrong thing in the wrong lane. Many of them still haven't figured out how to work their turn signals, let alone understand turn lanes. One thing you can count on, however, is that if your light has just turned green and you are going straight, someone with a red light will turn into your lane right in front of you.

On side streets in Concord, no one pays attention to the stop signs. Drivers taking side streets are often looking for a shortcut around town. They are not going to stop at fifteen intersections. Rumford and Merrimack on the west side of town are notorious for this problem. If you are driving on School or Warren, or any other street with lots of these types of intersections, proceed as if muggers are waiting for you at every corner. They probably are.

That's enough for today. Just remember that the key to survival is to maintain an even temperament. Don't let yourself succumb to impatience or road rage. I know I am quite proud of the way I have learned to deal with the road rage issue since a small incident that I had a few years ago. A black pickup cut me off down in Massachusetts when I was taking my 80-year-old mother shopping. I started chasing him through Wakefield, but I finally broke it off when we started to go down a side street and I noticed my mother whimpering and hiding under the glove compartment.

I haven't had any problem with that stuff in years. Come to think of it, my mother hasn't gone shopping with me in years either. ◆

Dumbing Down the Population

I BELIEVE IT IS A WASTE OF TIME to try to improve our educational system. The problem isn't with the schools . . . it is with the parents.

How can we expect the kids to be able to excel, when most of the parents have had their brains operating in the standby mode since before the kids were born.

Ever since the 1960s, we have been practicing a sort of "reverse Darwinism," whereby the public, fresh from frying their brains on drugs and alcohol, and tuning in to television on a regular basis, has gradually lost the ability to think. These people then mated with others of similar experience, and we suddenly had a new breed of child arriving on the planet. These children are immune to learning. I call it the "if Charlie Sheen married Paris Hilton, their kids would have trouble working a light switch" syndrome.

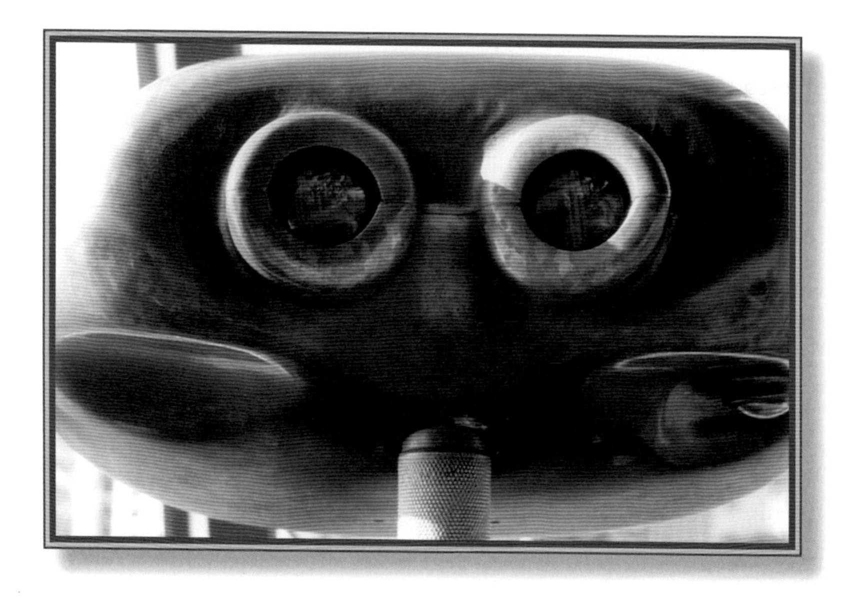

Now before you get too upset, I should clarify that I am definitely not talking about you or your children. The fact that you are reading this article clearly shows you are not in this group. No, I am referring to all those others out there who have demonstrated difficulty dealing with the simplest concepts, and have seemingly lost the ability to speak in sentences.

My theory on the rising level of stupidity of the general population is supported by the following:

A substantial number of voters in Florida recently raised a major issue over the difficulty of reading and filling out the "butterfly ballot." Since then, several tests of this ballot in grade schools have shown that fourth graders found this ballot to be easier to use than the water cooler. It has also been proven that a trained hamster, with good food incentives, could fill out this ballot successfully. What is the voter telling us?

When discussing the recent tax cut, the media has found it necessary to repeatedly tell us that those who don't pay taxes may not get much of a tax cut. This concept has apparently been so difficult to understand by the general populace, that reporters have felt the need to emphasize it ad nauseum. Let's study it one more time. *In order to really benefit from a tax cut, you may need to pay taxes.* Apparently this surprises a lot of our population. I imagine they are the same ones who rush down to the auto dealers every time a $1000 rebate is announced. The disappointment must be enormous when they find out that, to be eligible, they must first buy a car.

We have just witnessed the biggest speculative bubble in history by investors in "dot coms." We used to laugh at the idiots in Europe a few hundred years ago who threw away fortunes investing in tulip bulbs. Well guess what? We have proven ourselves to be even bigger idiots. We lost more money, and lost it quicker, and all we have to show for it is some bad paper. At least the tulip bulb investors could console themselves with some pretty flowers.

Even the general population itself, as represented by our class action lawyers, admits to being brain-challenged regarding cigarette smoking. We have all known for years that cigarettes were "coffin nails," and there have been labels on every cigarette pack for decades telling us that smoking was hazardous to our health. And yet we can still win lawsuits for $3 billion because we didn't realize those warnings could actually mean that smoking was bad for us. When the juries rule in favor of the smoker, what they are really saying is that Americans are too stupid to be responsible for their own decisions, and too dumb to read and understand the labels.

Finally, just turn on your TV and watch the doings of current celebrities like Britney Spears, Charlie Sheen and the inhabitants of *Jersey*

Shore. Hollywood, which many say reflects our society, has come a long way from the days of Jimmy Stewart, Katherine Hepburn and Lucille Ball, and the trip (no pun intended) has not been a productive one.

I could go on, but I think you get my point. The general population of this country has been defined by juries, the media, and the voters themselves, as incompetent nincompoops. Is it any wonder that the offspring of this population aren't winning the education sweepstakes?

So let's stop blaming the teachers, the school committees, and the textbooks. The bottom line is that we are fast becoming a nation of troglodytes, and our kids will be lucky if they can work a garden rake by the time we get through with them. ◆

Tourists

IT'S TOURIST SEASON AGAIN in New Hampshire. Or as we like to think of it, the chance to get people from somewhere else to help us pay all the bills that we can never figure out how to pay ourselves. Tourists are God's great gift to New Hampshire. They come here for our beautiful scenery, picturesque towns and quaint ways, and we find picturesque and quaint ways to take their money.

Many of these visitors say they come here because we're different. They want to experience life like it used to be, before the world was corrupted by things like reality television, concrete jungles and traffic jams. There is a certain disconnect in this of course. Many of them then check in to motels with satellite TV and swimming pools and video game rooms. And they all seem to flock to the same traffic-clogged, "scenic" highways and seek out places like Santa's Village.

Fortunately, we do still provide some opportunities for the hardier souls to return to the days when things were different. We have a fairly wide assortment of those cute little roadside cabins where people can see what it was like to live in a closet, and maybe meet some of our famous New Hampshire wildlife. (Ever wonder why many of those cabins are up on blocks?) We also have all sorts of colorful old antique shops where, if our visitors are tough enough to survive the dust and 1930s elevator music, they can buy back all the stuff they threw away twenty years ago. And for the truly adventuresome, we have attractions like the 139-year-old cog railway that climbs Mount Washington. In many ways this has not changed much since the 1800s. It provides tourists with a ride powered by authentic, coal-fired, smoke-spouting, steam engines (and one wimpy biodiesel engine), that will take them to perhaps the only place in New England where they can freeze their tail off in the middle of the summer.

Many of these tourists will also visit the wide variety of souvenir shops that are placed almost everywhere for their enjoyment. We are truly appreciative of their support, because without their amazing lack of taste, we would be stuck with all this stuff forever.

Other attractions that seem irresistible to tourists are the outlet malls that are scattered around the state. We provide a rustic ambience that induces people to buy clothes that went out of style five years ago in the rest of the country. They know they can get away with wearing it here because everyone gets away with wearing anything here. And when you throw in the special bonus of no sales tax on top of the discounts, we unload a lot of bargains.

Finally, for those tourists who are certifiable, and there seem to be a lot of them, we have our ocean beaches, where the water will turn their legs blue and their minds numb.

All things considered, we have good reason to love our tourists and welcome them back to our fine state. Just don't get yourself caught between them and the portable toilets on the Kancamagus Highway. ◆

Comments for a Wedding

MANY PEOPLE HAVE COMMENTED that they are amazed that someone as obnoxious and annoying as I am, has managed to stay married and alive for thirty years. Most of those people are members of my own family.

Given this accomplishment, Diana and Dave asked me to provide some guidance on how I managed this, apparently on the presumption that if I could do it, there is hope for everyone.

I guess my first words of advice would be to find a partner who can put up with you. This is not always easy, and generally requires superb powers of selection, and the good fortune to find someone with lots of patience and understanding. From what I have seen, I think Dave and Diana have got a good start on this. Dave seems to require a lot of patience and understanding, and Diana seems able to provide it.

The rest of my comments are more along the lines of a survivor's guide to marriage. And I will only burden you with a few words, since I have already provided Dave and Diana with a lengthy letter on the subject. Dave is learning early that developing a toleration for in-law advice is one of the first necessities of marriage.

I should also add that since these are from the husband's point of view, they may be more useful for men than women.

When your spouse is driving, keep your mouth shut unless your life is in danger, you are in the wrong state, or (unlikely) you are asked for help.

Don't criticize the way something is done unless you plan on doing it yourself . . . forever.

Remember, once in a while, to tell your spouse that she is right. This doesn't hurt too much, and sets the stage for proper recognition for all those times when you are right.

Foot rubs can get you out of a lot of trouble.

Don't goose your wife when she is watering the lawn.

When a question starts off with "What's more important?" there is only one right answer.

Take long walks together. It's a great time to communicate, and it keeps you from getting too fat.

Don't agree to anything until you have had your morning coffee.

There are exceptions to every rule.

There are some times when you need to turn off the ball game. ◆

A Walk in the Woods

THE LEAVES CRUMBLED under my feet. Everything else was so quiet that the sound of their distress reverberated along the path and well into the forest. The woods still carried some color, especially when contrasted with the rich blue of the sky. But the hiatus between foliage season and winter was clearly coming to an end and the air had a good bite to it.

I only jogged to the base of the hill. Even walking up to the water tower, it is easy to roll an ankle in the loose stones hidden under the leaves.

I turned at the tower and looked back across the town. The naked trees exposed a view that lay hidden in the summer. This morning a low fog had settled over the river and much of the valley. The sun was just above the far hill and skimmed its rays off the fog and through the trees, coming to rest in the heavy dew of the small field in front of me. The blades of grass sparkled, connected by a glistening net of silver webs.

I turned finally, moving past the tower and into the network of paths that meander all through the woods of west Concord. The distant sounds of traffic were muffled and then faded away. There remained only the noise of the leaves, the occasional bird that hadn't yet sought the warmth of southern climates, and a gentle whisper from the intermittent breeze.

I know these paths have been here for years, and I could feel the presence and kinship of those who have created and walked them before me: children playing capture the flag, old men reworking their regrets and recalls, couples finding their way together, and people walking their dogs. And on this particular morning, their was also a young woman jogger who was past me in a flash, and then disappeared down the path, moving strongly amid a light rustling of leaves and a trail of frozen breath.

I have named all the trails with which I am familiar. Foolish names based on rock formations and strange looking trees. But one path in particular intrigues me. This path moves fairly steeply down the back of the hill and I call it "steel wheel street." At one time it was more heavily traveled than many of the lesser-known real streets of Concord. Yet now it is at best a distant memory, even to many of the veterans of the Concord scene.

When I first walked it, I was intrigued by the obvious incidence of past activity. The primary indicators were the large steel wheels scattered along the path and down the hill. They were maybe two feet in diameter and were either pinned to trees or lying at various abandoned angles on the ground.

After making some inquiries, I learned that this area had been the site of a ski tow that St. Paul's had operated back in the '50s. It was apparently quite popular for a few years, and then was abandoned in favor of larger ski facilities that didn't require as much work getting up the hill and could take you on longer and more challenging trips down. Now only the wheels remain, lying as abandoned relics along a trail where the trees and undergrowth give doubt that a ski area ever existed. The "steel wheel" path is a gentle reminder that the woods that cover our state carry many messages about the origins of the land and the history of its settlement.

This network of paths exits at a wide variety of locations from Fisk Hill to Long Pond Road. I came out behind the Unitarian Church and jogged back up Pleasant Street to home. The approaching winter solstice was gradually pushing the sun lower in the sky, and warned of the coming months when the snow would hide this world from me. Even as it prepares to rest, however, it tells a story that lifts my spirits. ◆

Stop with the Choices, Already!

My wife won't let me go to the store with her. She says I take too long selecting purchases. She's right. The shopping world has become too complex for my tired brain to process.

Choices used to be relatively simple. If I wanted a candy bar, I would go to the store and pick one of about fifteen distinctive brands on the shelf. Now, in many of the drug stores and supermarkets, you have, literally, about two hundred different items on the shelves. One brand name, like Almond Joy, which used to be the Mounds bar with nuts, now comes in six or seven varieties. A Hershey chocolate bar has even more choices. I recently spent several minutes standing at the candy shelves at a supermarket trying to choose between a Passion Fruit Almond Joy and a Hershey's Dark Chocolate with Macadamia Nuts and Cranberry. A few hours later, after eating two of the Hershey Bars and half a box of Hot and Spicy Cheez-Its (ten kinds), I was back to purchase some Alka-Seltzer. Unfortunately, there are now fourteen different types of Alka-Seltzer. I spent so long making that choice that I then had to pick something for an aching back. I couldn't count all the choices on that one so I grabbed a bottle of aspirin and went home.

The same problems are out there with almost everything. There are now at least seven different kinds of Cheerios and six types of Centrum vitamin pills. Anheuser Busch appears to have a strategy to put out so many different brands of beer that they will crowd everyone else off the shelves.

It has all become too much. I moved to New Hampshire to keep things simple. This was the state with a motto of "Live Free or Die." What could be easier? How many choices does that take? We were a proud people that didn't mess around with all those gray half-choices. Our motto wasn't about some stupid state flower or how many lakes we had. We cut to the chase. If the country was going Communist, just nuke us and get it over. We certainly weren't a state getting hung up over eight different kinds of M&M's. Unfortunately, we crumbled before the corporate onslaught.

You can't even escape this stuff at home. I now have about three hundred channels on my TV and spend half my time surfing to see what I am missing (which is usually nothing). I get so tired working the clicker that I sometimes fall asleep in mid-click and wake up watching something like "Big(?) Losers." This in turn doubles their ratings, which is especially disconcerting because I then become partly responsible for keeping these losers on the air.

I know some of you are thinking, this guy is just getting old and can't make decisions anymore. And while I could concede that you have a point, I recently observed a similar problem encountered by a much younger citizen. I noticed a ten-year-old boy standing frozen in front of a major supermarket candy counter about a month ago. The kid had gone into some sort of hypnotic trance that left him totally unable to function for about twenty minutes. I later learned that his mother does that to him all the time. She brings him to the candy section and tells him he can just pick one, and then goes off and does her shopping.

I can envision a time in the not-too-distant future when we will all be that ten-year-old, frozen forever in indecision before the overwhelming number of choices in our lives. As for me, I am going to let my wife do the shopping and give up candy bars. From now on I am keeping it simple and eating healthy. Let's see, should I have the Special K with Red Berries, Protein Plus, Fruit and Yogurt or Vanilla Almond? ◆

Capital Offenses

One of the things that I really love about New Hampshire is that profligate living doesn't travel well up here.

In LA, if you build a big house on the top of a cliff overlooking the Pacific, everyone goes into a state of orgasmic ecstasy. No one seems to mind that the next big rainstorm may convert it into a beach house.

In New Hampshire, however, if someone builds an inaccessible home on a hilltop up a mile long driveway, the natives will spend the next twenty years laughing at the idiot, and imagining his plow bills and heating expenses when the wind is blowing and it's five degrees above zero. As cousin Shirley says, if I want to look at the damn view that bad, I can just climb up to the fire tower.

Actually, while we all want to have enough money, the really big money gets very impatient up here. There aren't that many ways to spend it. People have been known to use it to build private golf courses, but these can turn out to be so private that only the bankruptcy attorneys meet there. And putting together a huge wardrobe of designer original clothes doesn't impress much either. For many of us, a designer original is something you rig up to keep the pump working in flood season. Clothes, up here, especially in the winter, are just layers of fabric to keep out the cold and protect our butts when we slip on the ice.

Of course, the high livers can always buy several of those really expensive luxury cars, like a Rolls Royce or a Lamborghini, which will really look good in their garage all winter.

And speaking of garages, what about the houses some of these people are attaching to them. Old lake camps are getting torn down and replaced with ten bedroom mansions which are empty most of the year. The only impression it makes on us is a hearty thank you from the taxman for helping to keep taxes low for the rest of us. And a warm feeling knowing there is probably some other incredibly discerning individual out there who may pay us millions for our little camp when it comes time to sell.

Overall, I would say that the citizens don't impress easily up here. We surely do like the tourist money, and try to provide some real nice places for people to spend it. But if you are going to live up here, be prepared to lower the profile.

We still live with the old fashioned idea that money should be spent wisely, even if you have a lot of it. We don't need any darn fools running up the prices at the Turkey Farm or the Flying Goose or any of our other fancy restaurants. And we especially don't want any transplanted city slickers trying to make a fashion statement down at the bagel shop. ◆

Spelunking in Concord

The City Council recently decided to lower the speed limit on certain streets in Concord. This surprised me because in my part of town, we wish we could drive as fast as twenty-five miles per hour. If someone were that foolish, they would almost certainly wind up in someone's living room, or with a broken axle.

Yes, it is pothole season again, and we have grown some beauties this year. In some towns they grow pumpkins of unusual size; our specialties are craters and artificial mountains. With a little promotion, we could probably generate national fame. We certainly could swallow any of those pumpkins without even a hiccup.

I have read that Bow Brook runs along an earthquake fault. Perhaps this explains our unique capabilities in Concord. The shifting of tectonic plates are probably to blame for generating frost heaves the size of Appalachian foothills and sinkholes the size of small ponds.

Thanks to the frequent plowing of our roads, we have managed to avoid taking on the look of a junkyard, but I am confident that when spring comes and the snow (finally) melts, we will see the sides of the roads cluttered with broken wheels, hubcaps and tailpipe assemblies.

Some of you may remember the story of the submarine *San Francisco* running into an uncharted undersea mountain. I fear we have the same problem. Our road maps fail to show a whole range of land mountains that, if hit, could rearrange your fillings, or put you in a tree. Describing these things with a sign that says "bump," is like describing Kirstie Alley as "robust."

And I am pretty sure I have seen spelunkers being lowered into some of the caves on Mountain Road and Fruit Street. Rumor has it that the city is fast becoming a preferred destination for a variety of opportunists who are fascinated by the underground world opening up beneath our fair city. There is even talk that a high-grade vein of coal was found running underneath Washington Street and stretching all the way from North State to Westbourne. That would provide some nice tax help for the city. And a little open pit mining would hardly even be noticed on those roads.

I have also heard rumors that the city is about to ban small cars from some of these roads. There is apparently real concern that these vehicles could disappear forever in some of these caverns. At the very least, any cars smaller than 1977 Buicks should attach a red flag to the top of their antennas so that they may be more easily located by divers.

And finally, there is an uncorroborated story that a spelunker who went into a hole up near Ironworks Road came out under the Capital Center for the Arts. He apparently was able to ride an underground river into town and said he passed a VW Rabbit and a blue Mini on the way.

It has been another interesting season in the "pothole capital of the world." What the heck, let's claim credit where it's due. It could put us on the map like the pumpkin people. And maybe, in future years, we can host events like the world snowboarding championships. I noticed snowboarders doing some pretty fantastic loops off the moguls on upper Thayer Pond Road after the last storm. ◆

Notes from Eva Brown

One of the things that I enjoy about antique shops is imagining the individual stories that go with some of the items that are for sale. As a history buff, I particularly like prowling through old paper and other ephemera that show up occasionally. Sometimes I find something that provides a direct link to the original owner or issuer. Such was the case in Bedford a few months ago, when I came upon something that was directly traceable to the source, and also seemed relevant to the current discussions about the needs of our educational systems.

The item that caught my attention was a little "reward of merit" booklet that said "souvenir" on the cover. It was embossed with a picture in beautiful chromolithography that showed an open book on a bed of clouds. In the background were pictures of the torch of liberty, a quill pen and a drafting pencil. Below, on a marble pedestal, was written, "On every thorn, delightful wisdom grows. In every rill, a sweet instruction flows."

When I opened it, I learned that copies had been presented to her students by Eva Brown, a teacher at Eastern School in Danbury, in 1913. She had nine students, all listed in the booklet. The class appears to have been comprised of six boys and three girls. My guess, sexist though it may be, is that this paper booklet, surviving all these years in near mint condition, probably belonged to one of the girls.

The booklet contained two wonderful poems urging hard work, strong character, an appreciation of history, and the need to act in an honorable and moral way.

The current school systems, besieged at every turn by professional witch hunters, would probably never allow a teacher to issue this kind of booklet to students. The primary flaw is that the poems mention or allude to God and "heaven" in their content.

Since I am simplistic and not offended by references to God, I enjoyed them. I particularly liked the idea that they still emphasized the importance of history in our lives. This is a subject dear to my heart but which seems to be lost in the modern school systems. The first poem was written by G. Linnaeus Banks and is called "What I Live For." Here are a couple of the verses:

I live to learn their story,
Who suffered for my sake;
To emulate their glory,
And follow in their wake;
Bards, patriots, martyrs, sages,
The heroic of all ages,
Whose deeds crowd History's pages,
And times great volume make.
I live for those who love me,
And those who know me true,
For the Heaven that smiles above me,
And awaits my spirit too.
For the cause that lacks assistance,
For the wrong that needs resistance,
For the future in the distance,
And the good that I can do.

The second poem was called "Success" by John Froland. Here, also, I will only quote a couple of verses for fear of angering the sensitive. I fear that the message is now considered to be archaic thinking.

'Tis not the birth—its time or place—
To bar the power that waits on hope;
He wins who runs the strenuous race
Regardless of his horoscope.
Environment may lend a touch,
To round some angles to the plan,
But, for the finished work there's much,
Within the compass of the man.

As I read this simple little booklet, I thought how wonderful it was that a teacher cared enough to provide these to her students. The words told us a lot about how people used to deal with the education of our children in New Hampshire. But I also thought about how much trouble a teacher could get into in today's world if she were to hand out something like this.

Eva Brown left her students with some valuable guidance for living one's life, and a reminder to all of us of how dedicated and involved teachers could be in their stewardship of our children. It also provides a pretty good frame of reference for how far our modern schools have traveled away from those standards in the last hundred years.

In our efforts to say nothing offensive, it seems our teachers are now pushed into a position where they feel they can say nothing. I am not certain that in New Hampshire or in the country, the journey has been a productive one. ◆

The House

SUSANNE AND I are members of the population base that the media categorizes as the sandwich generation. As part of that, we are dealing with issues regarding our parents and their needs. One particular aspect of this is proving to be a truly daunting task: the cleaning out of the family residence.

Someday, in the distant future, scientists will extract clues as to the nature of our civilization from the content of our homes. But, in the present, those of us uneducated in the skills of archaeology are required to wing it as we fulfill an obligation to our parents and, in the process, uncover layer after layer of our ancestral heritage.

My wife is actually doing most of the true archaeological digging since I suffer from a variety of maladies that make it impossible to remain on the scene for more than a few minutes at a time. I have found that longer stays reduce me to a whimpering mass of dyspeptic DNA, incapable of coherent sentences and subject to hot flashes and fits of psychotic laughter.

My childhood home, as I used to think of it, has been in the family for more than eighty years. Since my parents moved out a few months ago and sought the sanctity of an independent living facility, however, it has become known as simply "the house."

My parents were right to move out. It is a large house and carried the weight of three generations. Life is simpler and the burdens fewer in the new location. What remains, however, is a task of such complexity, and so physically and emotionally overwhelming that it has brought many of us lesser souls to our knees. Fortunately, my wife perseveres, with a minimum of help from the rest of us, and we have managed to slowly uncover several layers of this representative piece of civilization. I thought it might be useful to provide those of you who have yet to experience this particular task with a sample of what may come. For convenience, I have broken the stages of discovery into descriptive subsets.

The Nuclear Attack Food Stockpile. Masks were definitely needed for this dig. We went into the basement storage room *en masse* (help was enlisted from my sister, brother-in-law and niece). The expedition was well planned and executed, and we removed about sixteen bags of canned and packaged food, old vegetables, and various unrecognizable items. Much of this could be traced back to the Reagan era, through carbon dating techniques. We escaped with only minor casualties and the need for general inhalation therapy. I have not, however, been able to persuade my sister and her family to return from California since that memorable event.

The Plant Problem. My mother has a green thumb that is perhaps unmatched in modern times. Everything grows in her house. Even when she isn't there. While we were getting my folks settled, and screwing up our courage for another run at "the house," the plants took over four rooms. It was actually pretty scary. They didn't seem to need water, and they were growing at record rates. After several months of fear and indecision, I finally persuaded Susanne to do a plant evacuation. I guess it was pretty brutal. Some of the plants didn't want to leave voluntarily, and clung tenaciously to the furniture and light fixtures. Gloves were definitely needed for this one. I still have nightmares about those cactus guys and the vine things.

The Media Graveyard. We are still in the removal stage for perhaps the world's largest collection of old magazines, newspapers, sweepstakes mailings and junk mail. I believe that these things procreate when left alone together. I am particularly suspicious of an affair between the *Redbook* and the *Rotarian* magazines, although I think the *McCalls* are also fooling around. Every time we think we have dealt with this issue effectively, we find new hiding places. Recently, I made the mistake of going to the attic, and was viciously assaulted by a cascading pile of *Time* magazines.

The Clothes Crisis. There are at least three rooms in "the house" that have been inaccessible for several years because of an excess supply of old clothes. The variety is amazing. There are old uniforms, suits, vintage wear, WT Grant modern, double knit, rayon, peg-legged, flared, long, short, Hawaiian, Madras, adult, child, summer, winter, and a general catch-all category that I define as eclectic. It is, in truth, a fascinating example of one family's 20th century clothes odyssey. We haven't really begun to deal with this yet. This area is particularly frightening to my wife, because she knows I will probably try to add some of the items to my wardrobe.

The Household Esoterica Collection. This is the last area I am going to deal with here. And I must preface my remarks by saying that my folks collected some truly wonderful things over the years, which we are delighted that they have saved for our families. They also, however, apparently were intrigued by the bizarre and unusual in everyday inventions. And these are what I am including in this category. Most of these items have been kept in mint, still in the package, condition and are a source of wonder and amazement. We recognize their value in any study of our civilization; we just don't know what to do with them. I am simply going to list a few to give you a feel of the scope of the conundrum. The Condiment Helper (serves honey and syrup without dripping). The Clip-on Pill Caddy (great for pocket or purse, looks like a fat pen). Dust Grabber Broom Cover (covers the action part of a broom). ThermaLock Cordless Electric Bag Sealer. Dessert Divider (equal portions every time, but very small portions since the 10-way circular divider is only four inches in diameter). Sock Saver (never lose socks again). Manicure Mate (achieve nail salon results every time). Belt Organizer (instantly organizes up to thirteen belts, a nice round number). The 5-Way Super Food Slicer (for when you really want to slice and dice). I guess that's enough. Most of these items are not available in any store.

We are far from finished with this assignment. Most of the rooms are still untouched and we haven't begun to face the attic and basement (except for the nuclear stockpile and an unplugged extra refrigerator that I was unfortunate enough to open). I am sure there will be many more stages in our archaeological dig. In some ways I guess it is coming to terms with my past. Somebody told me that when I finally had to do that, it might be a painful and emotionally draining experience. I guess I just never realized the pain would take quite this form. This is an experience I plan to share with my kids, however, and so I am actively working at accumulating my own stockpile of eclectic stuff. Someday, they will have to deal with these same issues, and I will take some satisfaction in the knowledge that I got even. I suggest that the rest of you also plan accordingly. ◆

Surviving on the Roads

My youngest daughter has just turned sixteen. The significance of this is not lost on anyone who has teenagers. It is independence day. It is also the day that parents see their offspring begin to be turned loose into that vast sea of motorists. It doesn't take much imagination to be a little concerned for anyone facing the snarling crowd that drives the American roads.

We have worked hard to try to prepare her to be a careful and considerate driver. She has gone through the school's driver education program, and has been lectured by us on defensive and situational driving so much that she can name and number each speech even before we know we are giving it.

Even with all this preparation, however, those of us who have been driving for a few years know that "it's a jungle out there." There are some aspects of this new world for which no amount of instruction and practice can prepare you. Ultimately, it takes luck, good survival skills, experience and a little weird science to successfully deal with the world that you meet behind the wheel. I have tried to explain that to my daughter, but she is a budding scientist and there is no way to quantify it.

I decided therefore to try to list a few of the gray areas in which she could at least benefit from fair warning about what she might encounter. One area where I felt comment might be useful relates to understanding the way people communicate when they get behind the wheel. A simple example is the interpretation of flashing highbeams during daylight. This action can have several meanings, including (1) speed trap ahead (2) hello (3) nice taste in cars (usually because it is like your own) (4) you are going to slow, let me pass and (5) oops, I was trying to turn on the windshield wipers. The experienced driver knows that, unless positive, he/she should always assume number (1).

There are many other methods that are used by drivers to communicate. This is partly a result of the tendency of people to become much more frank and expressive when they get behind the wheel. A strange transformation takes place that converts Pee Wee Herman into Godzilla and Aunt Mini into Kathy Bates. These drivers have no hesitancy in alerting you to perceived shortcomings in your driving style. This can be done by any combination of horn, internationally known hand signals, and if the window is down, an occasional complex series of hyphenated, multi-syllabic, verbal instructions that may or may not be physically possible. Young drivers are not always certain of the correct response to these instructions. Years of experience tells us that no response is usually best. Especially if it's a pickup truck with a gun rack, or the driver has multiple tattoos on his face and shoulders.

The new driver will also find, however, that people are willing to share much more of their personal life with you when they are on the road. One way this is done is through the use of bumper stickers. Sometimes you can even develop dangerous tailgating habits trying to read them all. Astute observers can learn about another driver's occupation, sexual persuasion and preferences, philosophy of life, religion, status of car payments, political outlook, special interest group affiliations, college, sport preferences and number of grandchildren. Sometimes all of this is provided on one car. My favorite was a sticker loaded car that had, as its centerpiece, the following: "Men are idiots and I married their king." I learned more about that person in the timing of one red light than I know about neighbors that have lived next to me for ten years.

There is a down side to this, however. A new driver is generally not aware of the disturbing correlation that appears to exist between the number of bumper stickers, and the tendency for the car to be driven erratically. My personal theory for this is that a large number of stickers are often used as the modern equivalent of baling wire and they are probably holding the car together. I usually treat these cars as moving time bombs and assume that either the car or driver may come apart momentarily.

Another rule of the road that is difficult to teach young drivers is to give a wide berth to all pickup trucks. Operators of these vehicles should be presumed crazy until proven otherwise. I realize that this is a pretty broad statement, and I even have a couple of friends who drive these things who I would consider borderline sane, but, in general, keep two lanes between you and these vehicles until you determine the level of insanity you are facing. Be especially on the lookout for any of the following characteristics:

If the driver requires a stepladder to get into his vehicle.

If the truck actually has a rifle in the gun rack.

If there are dobermans, pit bulls or wild animals running loose in the truck bed.

If they bounce more than one empty beer can off your windshield.

Experienced drivers know that when encountering any of these situations, they should immediately seek alternative travel routes. And in the case of the last example in combination with any of the first three, you should proceed to the nearest donut shop and seek police protection.

Another lesson that only comes from experience is the ability to properly read and interpret license plates. Generally, vanity plates should be a warning indicator. Experience will eventually teach young drivers that plates that describe body parts, social status, criminal convictions or an alcoholic beverage are caution lights. Plates from Texas, California and New York should also be a cause for concern. Massachusetts is in a category by itself. The New Hampshire legislature could do young drivers a great service if they required that a mandatory label be put on every driver's license that reads: "Caution: Massachusetts drivers can be hazardous to your health."

There are dozens of other lessons on driving life that could benefit young operators, but we all seem to have to learn those the hard way. Schools can't teach them and kids generally wouldn't listen anyway. When you think about it, if new drivers really knew what was out there, or believed you when you described it, they would be riding the bus.

Kids are going to keep heading out there, however, and all we can do is try to be supportive and repetitious. Come to think of it, there are still a few things I can teach her, like the correlation between lack of driving skills and the number of things hanging off the rearview mirror, and what to do when you see the guy in front of you with both arms wrapped around his girlfriend . . . or you suddenly can't see his girlfriend . . . ◆

Our Northern Border

Most of us who live in New Hampshire don't spend a lot of time worrying about our northern border. It's just one of those things that has always been there and has seemed to work okay. We have lots of other stuff to fret about and very few migrant workers are sneaking across the border to take jobs in the North Country.

Nevertheless, with all the drug smuggling and terrorist worries, I was interested to see a recent article that indicated that Canada is finally taking its border responsibilities seriously. The article in the *Washington Post* and later picked up locally, focused on an announcement by Prime Minister Stephen Harper that Canada will soon begin a program to arm its border guards.

I guess this is welcome news. Apparently the border guards were previously expected to stand their ground against drug smugglers, carloads of terrorists, crazed serial killers and other bad guys, armed only with pepper spray and batons. Needless to say, there was some concern that if suicidal terrorists, or big budget drug dealers, pulled out their AK-47s, Uzis and antitank weapons in a confrontation, the border guards, no matter how brave, might have had an inclination to vacate the area. But now, the border guards will be armed with handguns. This should make all the difference. One puzzling part about the announcement of this bold step, however, is that it will take ten years to accomplish. Apparently, the training program for the use of these complex weapons is not up to speed. The first 150 of the 4400 guards were armed by March of 2008, followed by about 500 more each year.

Still, I guess it's the thought that counts. Canada has acknowledged that it's a dangerous world out there and is showing itself ready to confront the terrorist and criminal threats in a forthright manner that seems typical of enlightened governments everywhere. The guards may not be quite as excited. The good news is that they had one out of every thirty officers armed with some kind of weapon by 2008. The bad news is that twenty-nine out of every thirty guards were still armed with pepper spray. Maybe that is why the extensive need for training. If you're the lucky one with a handgun, and you're facing off against an AK-47 or an antitank weapon, you better be a really good shot. I also wouldn't count heavily on the pepper spray backup from your fellow guards.

Even though I know that this step is well-intentioned, I am not certain that such a bold move actually causes less stress among New Hampshire citizens. Personally, the pepper spray armament that existed was information I didn't want to know. And maybe we didn't want to tell the nuclear terrorists that, even now, the worst case scenario for a border confrontation from the Canadian guards involves stinging eyes and some savage baton dents on the fenders of their rental car, augmented by an occasional pistol. ♦

Empty Bedrooms

My daughters' rooms are empty now. And the emptiness is different from college days, when there was still a scattering of the small treasures of childhood that indicated a planned return.

Yes, there are still a few items that signify their presence, their attachment to this place. But the details, the everyday evidence of their lives, are now elsewhere.

My study is filled with mementos of their progression through two and a half decades of our lives. Smiling pictures, a pair of well-used, size 3, Big Smith overalls, handmade birthday cards, a machine-tooled piece of metal, and team-signed softballs from their glory days.

Now, however, they are involved in new beginnings, living their lives in this unpredictable, wonderful, scary, beautiful, dangerous, challenging world.

They were each married this year, and they will soon be living in equally distant places, halfway across the country. And I am so happy for them, as they find their own way in their lives, and as we become a part of a larger family.

Things are different now for us as well. As I sit by my window, looking out at the incredible array of reds and oranges and yellows and greens, I can't help but feel that perhaps this year, I am a participant in, rather than just a watcher of, the change in season. As parents, our lives are also entering a new period, and there is a much more acute sense of the mixed emotions that have always seemed such an integral part of the arrival of autumn.

My purpose in writing this is not, however, to lament this change. I know that November and December will bring grayer days, but that they will also bring some sunshine and beauty. Instead, I am taking this occasion, with New Hampshire in its best dress, to celebrate something that we did right.

Some things in life, you learn in time. And I am thankful that, as a family, we decided fifteen years ago, to move back to New Hampshire, and take the time to watch our daughters grow up.

Through all those changing seasons, we were able to share our lives. As a family we lived through the disappointments, and worries, and the triumphs of their progression to adulthood. It wasn't always a smooth journey, but then it probably never is for any family. But, as parents, we were there to watch the accomplishments, and provide the hugs that sheltered them against the cold realities of the world. And we laughed and cried together. And we grew older together. And that was what we wanted.

I know that one family's choice is probably irrelevant to many. We are all constantly faced with setting priorities and making choices. And there are some families that have successfully dealt with the conflicts of high-powered careers and family needs. I learned that I couldn't. Perhaps more importantly, our family realized this soon enough to change things, and that has made all the difference.

And now, when I look back at those years, I do it with some sadness that they are gone, and with a sense of melancholy about how fast our lives travel across time. But I also have a sense of satisfaction that we did the best that we could with those years, and that we made the right decisions, for us, in grabbing hold of those moments when they were offered to us.

It makes it a little easier, as I walk through the empty bedrooms, and watch the leaves get carried by the wind, into the early October evening. ◆

The Art of Christmas

THERE HAVE BEEN LOTS OF GRINCHES out there the last few weeks, telling us why we are all idiots for having the temerity to use our imaginations during this Christmas season.

We see frequent articles and letters criticizing the folly of those who disagree with "established science" and what it can tell us about the birth of Christ and creation. For good measure they toss in critiques of Santa Claus as well. It seems that those who have all the answers, can't wait to share them with all of us pathetic fools who buy Christmas trees, rejoice in hope and gather together to share the joy of our beliefs.

Perhaps we all need to take a step back and develop a little perspective about "established science." Science, through the ages, has been just like politics and religion, in that those in power believe they have all the answers and consider it a grievous affront for anyone to take issue with their boundless wisdom.

It was the "established" scientific community that decreed the world was flat, the Sun revolved around the Earth, heavier-than-air machines could not fly, the platypus could not exist, and no one could really throw a curve ball (it was an optical illusion). And they didn't come running with early acclaim for Einstein or Edison either. Almost every major scientific advance came only after withering criticism or disbelief by those with all the answers. The new discoveries were advanced by people who had questions and imagination and a willingness to admit that there are many possibilities in the universe.

Today we see much the same thing happening. It is a human condition, I guess, for those with a little intelligence to often decide they have a lot of intelligence, and appoint themselves the arbiters of all things possible. We still see it in politics and religion, and we certainly see it in science.

We also see it too often in the news. If something cannot be proven "scientifically," it is discarded as the raving of lunatics. Perhaps this is very similar to the treatment that would have occurred one thousand years ago if someone had started talking about the internet or cell phones or electricity. In those days such rantings would probably have gotten you burned at the stake. Today the punishment is more humane. Individuals are just pilloried with ridicule and scorn if they let their imagination soar into areas like the mysteries of creation. Those with all the answers have shown no real love for inquisitive minds or goodwill toward men.

It is frankly astonishing to me to see how agitated some in the scientific community get when someone implies that there are certain things that may be beyond all our understanding. They lash out with vituperation and personal assault, demanding that absolute proof be provided for every belief.

If a bumblebee were forced to prove he could fly, he would probably never make it off the ground. Sometimes, it takes a little faith. But unproven theories are the beginnings of all the great discoveries. And new revelations confound "established science" with great frequency. It has been a mix of imagination, wonder and a little humility, along with intelligence, curiosity and persistence that has led to most of the great discoveries in history. In all areas of religion, politics and science, the great minds needed to be able to see beyond the "established" thinking of their times.

Perhaps someday there will be another revelation for those with all the answers. Until that time, however, maybe these people could take a break. Why not take a nice vacation with those foolish days off that you have received. And give those of us who still take some things on faith the chance to enjoy the wonders and the joys of this season. Let us give wings to our imagination and our exploration of the secrets of the universe, and let our children still enjoy the excitement of Santa Claus. Mostly, just give us all a chance to relax in the pleasure of loved ones and share the gifts that we give and have been given.

And maybe all of us can take a moment to step outside on a cold starry night and reflect on the wisdom of thinking we have all the answers. ◆

God Save Us

Time magazine recently had a cover story indicating that there were only 648 days until the election. And candidates are showing up everywhere. It's like that "whack-a-mole" game at the arcade. Every time you blink, another head pops up. And there aren't enough mallets to make them go away.

Personally, I buy into the theory that anyone foolish enough to want to be President, is too stupid to deserve the job.

What can these people be thinking? If you get elected, you have no privacy, you have to deal with some of the biggest hypocrites on Earth (other politicians), and you have to make decisions which will be considered "wrong-headed" by at least one hundred and fifty million people. And that's just in this country.

If you are a Republican, you will be depicted as a heartless idiot who played football without a helmet or is about to turn the world into a nuclear wasteland.

If you are a Democrat, you become an irresolute wimp who will need an advisor to tell you what to have for breakfast. You will be the one who never had a real job, and wants to steal money from the mouths of those who do.

If elected, you will be criticized every time you eat a cheeseburger or take a vacation. You will be highlighted on the evening news whenever you trip on the stairs, spill coffee on your shirt, mispronounce a name or fall asleep during some speech that would send the rest of us into a coma.

Your family will be the prey of attack dogs. Your kids will be a national topic every time they get a speeding ticket, use a fake ID or sneak into the rose garden for a cigarette. Your wife will be analyzed regarding her clothing whenever she makes a public appearance. If she chooses not to be a fashion model, but actually still wants to have a life, she will be vilified for her selfish choices.

You will be hounded relentlessly by newspeople, many of whom bring no perspective to life other than how to work a microphone. And you will be the target of a million blogs trying to destroy you.

As a candidate, you will be forced to prostitute yourself to the media and the providers of dollars.

Republicans will be assaulted with threats and advice from evangelists, corporate lobbyists, single-issue right-wing nuts, and people who think the key to international relations is to "nuke the bastards."

If you are a Democrat, you will be advised by single-issue left wing nuts, foreign billionaires, celebrities like Paris Hilton and Alec Baldwin, and people who think the way to handle terrorists is to invite them into your kitchen for cake and cookies.

And when it is over, what happens to the losers? Some of them run over and over, like lost souls in some bizarre version of *Groundhog Day*. Others become purveyors for Viagra, start speaking in tongues, or withdraw into worlds where they are irrelevant, but nobody cares enough to tell them.

Overall, the rewards don't seem that great. Still, this season even more than most, we are faced with a proliferation of masochists. And for them, the prize will be even tougher than usual. Not only will they have to bankrupt themselves, both literally and figuratively, but they will need to do it for two full years. And they will also have to spend a lot of time, not only in wintry New Hampshire and the plains of Iowa, but they will have to wander that vast wasteland known as Nevada.

God save us all. ◆

Adultery Tax

Recently, I was having coffee with a friend who pointed out one of the headlines in the *Concord Monitor*. It was a reference to the current attempt in the legislature to do away with the statute on New Hampshire's books that makes adultery illegal.

She was adamant that instead of eliminating it, we should use it as a source of revenue. The more I thought about it, the more I became convinced that she was right. A few years ago, I wrote a piece for the *Monitor* proposing that we institute a "lying politicians" tax in the state. This would have been imposed on all politicians, state and national, who ran for office in the state. It imposed a fee on each politician who was caught in a lie. (Different levels of fines applied, depending on the magnitude of the lie.) If the legislature had taken my advice, a conservative estimate indicates that we would now have a fully funded pension system and a budget surplus.

It is entirely feasible that an "adultery tax" could raise almost as much revenue. It might be a little tricky to collect, but I think it could be done. Here is how:

Put an extra 10 percent room tax on all hotels and motels, just on the assumption that at least 10 percent of users are engaged in this activity. (I realize this is probably unreasonably low, but I want to be fair to the motel owners.)

Every time a divorce is finalized in the state, we could charge a $200.00 "what were you thinking?" fee. It is estimated that at least half of these were probably caused by adultery and we (the state) might as well benefit from the misfortune. Think of it as a public service head slap, and a nice source of revenue.

We could authorize our police forces to immediately write "adultery accusation" tickets every time they answer a domestic dispute in which this subject comes up. This ticket would be a fine of $100.00, but if the accusing party could prove the accusation was true, then the ticket would be voided and the offending party would be hit with a $1000.00 fine.

In fairness to frequent offenders, it also might be useful to offer "season passes" that could be sold at the same places that now offer hunting and fishing licenses. These passes would exempt offenders from all the other adultery fines. An additional benefit of this would be that the miscreant could then show his aggrieved spouse that the whole issue was moot because he had a "season pass." This argument might best be put forth in a crowded place well away from access to firearms.

I think the state has been negligent in its efforts to find new sources of revenue. We seem to place our taxes on the good things people do, like buying and selling homes, earning a living and driving cars. Instead, we should be taxing them for the bad things, like doing drugs, causing an accident, and cheating on a spouse or at golf (now there's a potential moneymaker).

I am estimating that if we combined an "adultery tax" with my previously recommended "lying politicians tax," and took it nationwide, we could generate enough revenue to eliminate the national debt. ◆

Style Issues

I AM, ADMITTEDLY, not an expert on style and fashion trends. I wear plaid shirts in the winter, chinos and golf shirts in the summer, and my color choices are usually dictated by what is on top of the pile. My wife has to use trickery to get me into a clothing store.

As an uneducated, fashion Neanderthal, I feel I am in the perfect position to comment on what the rest of you have chosen to wear. After all, I am not conflicted by allegiance to anything that could remotely be called style.

I have chosen to do this because I am tired of having my senses assaulted by a steady stream of eye pollution that crushes both my libido and my appetite.

Ladies, the lowrider-pants look is good on about five percent of the female population. Most of them are under twenty. Many of the rest of you are instead achieving the lowrider-plumber look. Trust me when I tell you that a red thong is not that attractive when it peeks out over a butt crack the size of the Grand Canyon.

But the problem actually gets much worse. The other day I saw a woman who must have wedged herself into some lowrider jean shorts with the jaws of life. She had made her belly button disappear deep within the enormous folds of a front butt crack. If it hadn't been for the copious cleavage spilling out of her blouse, you would not have been able to tell if she was coming or going. This look is hazardous to pedestrians who have no idea which way to run.

Another style item that is becoming increasingly popular with teenage girls is the permanent clothing option called "the big tattoo." Girls used to be satisfied with little tattoos to assert their independence: a tiny butterfly in a secret place or a little barbed wire around the arm to bring out their feminine charm. But lately, I have seen youngsters going for huge, full color "tats," covering their back or stomach or chest. I am struck by the sense of commitment to style that this represents. My experience with teenage girls (two daughters and their friends) was that they can change their minds, hairstyles and clothes, several times in a day. I would estimate that by the time they are twenty, they have probably made about 15,000 fashion choices. I wonder if that sixteen inch dragon across her back will always be the style of choice.

Of course, with men, the general situation is much worse. Women's styles change frequently, so that there is always hope that a bad look will die a quick death. But with guys, the looks seem to last interminably. Take the "rapper" look that has been around so very, very, very long with teenage boys. The full statement here includes 1) "load-in-the-pants" trousers with the crotch down to the knees, 2) sneakers the size of Mini-Coopers, 3) athletic jerseys thankfully down to the knees to hide what the trousers forgot, and 4) baseball hats worn in the universal method to declare to the world "look at me, I am as dumb as a fence post." This look has worked for years to keep these kids from getting any kind of gainful employment. I would also think it might hinder any kind of athletic endeavors, since running in those pants and sneakers would be sure to lead to unpleasant injuries.

Some male baby boomers are also responsible for perpetuating particularly unattractive styles. The perennial comb-overs and bad rugs are one thing, but the more recent hit with the well-to-do older generation is the "drug-dealer do." Once upon a time, Antonio Banderas, or some other minimalist actor, put his hair in a ponytail. Shortly thereafter, every Hollywood drug dealer and over the hill producer decided this style was them. Ultimately, and for too, too long, it spread to a significant number of balding, aging, midlife crisis baby boomers who think it makes them look like Banderas. Gentlemen, this look may work for guys who actually have hair, and also for those few who have worn it nonstop from the days when they actually lived on the commune. But for the rest of you, the message is more like, "capitalist pig having a midlife crisis."

Okay, I'm sorry I got so worked up. It was actually the emotional trauma caused by the lady with the two-way butt crack that did it. But I do understand that we all should be free to make our own fashion statements, no matter how frightening or unnerving. And today's fashions may seem mild compared to what designers dream up next. I was reminded of this just the other day when I was in Maine watching NESN. A local ad came on in which an aging, bald, furniture salesman, with lots of hair on his chest, appeared wearing a woman's two piece bikini. The impact of this image was so overwhelming that I didn't even notice if he was wearing a ponytail. ◆

Rolling with the Times

I AM CONTINUALLY FASCINATED by the resourcefulness of our capitalist system. It has been so successful that many people in this country have all the basic essentials and a wide variety of extras. Yet there seems to be no limit in the quest by some of our corporations and our citizens to explore new frontiers in innovative consumption.

Since we in New Hampshire have always been known to be among the nation's fashion and technology leaders, I thought you might benefit from a brief synopsis of some of the more interesting of these actual new inventions.

The toilet roll extender and supersized rolls. I just got a free extender delivered with my newspaper. This promises to be the greatest breakthrough in this field since the introduction of the Ayatollah Khomeini toilet paper roll (which took political commentary to a different level). This new addition to the toilet pantheon requires some minor installation, but promises to save the average family somewhere between 48 and 60 seconds a year in replacement time. A bonus benefit is that with even larger rolls of paper, your four-year-old will have additional resources at his disposal as he explores the new world of toilet flushing.

The microbe-killing countertop. (The Silestone by Cosentino USA.) This is apparently available for those with a good imagination. No one is quite sure what microbes are killed, but it is pretty certain they aren't the ones that make people ill. However, this probably provides great peace of mind to both family and visitors to know the kitchen counter is killing microbes 24/7. It seems to me that what this country really needs is something a little more powerful. But there may be a few marketing problems and less reassurance for family and friends if you mention you just installed a roach-killing countertop.

The Suck-it-Up automatic wheel cleaner. (From GrimeTech.) Apparently dirty wheels on our cars are the next great grime crime. Fortunately, you can purchase and install an automatic filtration system to keep your wheels and tires clean. It uses filters that need to be replaced as often as you change your oil. In New Hampshire, of course, this is not as big a problem as in some states because we have our own wheel cleaners . . . called potholes. These not only knock the dirt off, but sometimes the wheels as well. This presents some interesting possibilities, however. In places like Hollywood and Palm Springs, the citizens will be paying $340 plus replacement filters to keep their wheels free from dirt and grime with the Suck-it-Up. Perhaps New Hampshire could develop an export market for our potholes. For a much lower price, our Department of Transportation could probably install a genuine New Hampshire pothole right in front of their driveway that will knock almost anything off their car.

If you are actually thinking about any of these products, I suggest you hold off on your purchase and wait for the second generation to come out. I have already heard rumors that scientists are working on a combination product that would be a must in every New Hampshire household: the microbe-killing, self-cleaning, supersized roll of toilet paper. ◆

Goodbye Old Man

So THE OLD MAN is gone. The symbol of New Hampshire has been ground down by the wind and rain and snow and ice, and has finally left us. Perhaps this last long winter was just too much, although I prefer to think that it was an accumulated onslaught from thousands of New Hampshire winters.

My first memories of him were from a visit when I was about seven or eight. Our family had traveled up to Franconia Notch from the White Lake campgrounds, and we stopped for a very cold swim in the lake below. My parents said the water was so cold because the Old Man's winter blanket was made of snow that melted in the spring and filled the lake. That certainly seemed to fit the Old Man's image as I perceived it. He didn't look very warm and fuzzy. He appeared hard-nosed (literally) and no-nonsense, and the water below reflected that personality.

As I spent more time in the state, however, I grew to appreciate his stern, unblinking adherence to the values that have become a trademark of the New Hampshire native. His countenance on our license plates under the words "live free or die" seemed just right. He seemed to announce to the world that New Hampshire was different. He peered out at us with an independence and strength and fortitude that spoke for and to our citizens.

A verse from an old Dartmouth song, ("The Men of Dartmouth," by Richard Hovey) referred to its alumni—naturalized New Hampshire citizens all—as having "the still north in their souls, and the hill-winds in their breath." This seemed to me to describe no one better than the Old Man. He stood there for all those many years, an unshakable guardian of the northern passes. And he sent an enduring message to all who ventured into this country that this was someplace special. A land of beauty, and perseverance, and hardscrabble living and old-fashioned values.

There are rumors about trying to do some kind of salvage or reconstruction of the Old Man. I hope that talk is wrong. He doesn't deserve to become some kind of plastic tourist attraction, filled with glue and stuffing. He toughed it out pretty good in his final years. He weathered the elements in intensive care with the help of cable bandages and lots of nursing. But now he has finally returned to the dust that claims all things. He should be allowed to rest in peace. ◆